COLORADO
ANTIQUE LOVER'S GUIDE

EDITED BY NIKI HAYDEN
FRONT RANGE LIVING

FULCRUM PUBLISHING
GOLDEN, COLORADO

ISBN 1-55591-493-4
ISSN 1544-3787

Editorial: Marlene Blessing, Daniel Forrest-Bank, Alison Auch
Cover and interior design: Anne Clark

Printed in Singapore
0 9 8 7 6 5 4 3 2 1

Fulcrum Publishing
16100 Table Mountain Parkway, Suite 300
Golden, Colorado 80403
(800) 992-2908 • (303) 277-1623
www.fulcrum-books.com

CONTENTS

When I first met with the original writers at Front Range Living nearly three years ago, most of us had arrived from the world of Colorado newspapers. All of us had experience covering the daily stories of everyday life and we wanted to continue to do so—but in a different arena with a new slant. Together we hammered out the areas that we believed were of compelling interest to readers. One was the cultural world of history, design, and architecture. The other was the natural world, whether cultivated in gardens or visited on a mountainside.

We pooled our ideas and came up with a philosophy for covering the immense and spectacular terrain of Colorado. And while there are magazines devoted to environmental concerns and books devoted to extreme sports, we imagined chapters more personal, almost like a diary.

"Animals," said Dianne Zuckerman, who has always championed the feathered and furred. For this former theater critic for newspapers and magazines, the natural world is a tooth-and-claw stage, full of crises and struggles, winners and losers.

"Leisure and fun, too," said Beth Krodel, who loves to soak in a hot springs after a day of hiking. Following a stint as a foreign correspondent in the Middle East, Beth is content to find adventure closer to home.

"Learning about the rocks, plants, and land formations," was my response. No one can overlook our spectacular rocks, but I wanted to write about the smaller worlds, too—the delicate pasque flower with petals as thin as tissue, the migration of butterflies in mid-July, and the call of birds that flock around Barr Lake.

We would take our readers on journeys into our wide-open spaces and ask questions that any ordinary person might ask. And then we would report back. Not one of us is a scientist or an Olympic athlete. We would search for outdoor experiences that anyone would enjoy. And in most cases, these would be trips on which you could take a child, mother, neighbor, or friend.

When Carol Ward and I sat down to discuss how best to cover antiques in Colorado, we came with similar perspectives. We wanted to introduce our readers to the joys—and caveats—of collecting. Whether you crave the rustic lodge look or the frills of Victoriana, we would search for solid information. "Old World elegance," Carol, who loves the country styles of Europe, said, "History as it is handed down in objects and places or a prized possession that tells a story." Together we have searched for stories that cover Colorado uniquely: our love for all things Western, casual interiors that mix the old with the new, appreciation of workmanship and craft, glassware, jewelry styles, or silver serving utensils that never will be made again.

In doing so, we talked to dealers who have become experts in their fields and to collectors who have amassed a valuable group, or, more often, simply indulged in an affordable passion. Antiques are linked to our cultural history and reveal the abrupt changes in our homes, children's playthings, dining habits, entertainment, and fashion.

If antique stories divulge the small details of the past, homes and gardens tell volumes. Houses from previous generations reveal not only the strata of the wealthy and working classes, but also the dominant art of the day: arts and crafts, English Tudor, Spanish adobe, Victorian neo-Gothic. Gardens, too, are linked to the buildings they surround, like petticoats enhancing the prima ballerina. Colorado contains the comfortably worn and the cutting-edge. Heidi Anderson and I searched for old and new, grand and modest, historical and modern. Where she found recycled, renewable, revamped architecture, I found familiarity in bungalows, Victorians, and modernist design.

Gardening brings a history through the decades as well. Before drought gripped Colorado, scientists voiced concern that we were stretching our water supplies. Living in a semiarid climate, coupled with the influx of new residents, makes water conservation a hot topic for gardeners. The answer to wise planting may be in native plants that predate any people at all. Or, perhaps the old-fashioned plants that have survived adverse conditions over many decades will shape our landscape. Then, there are the newer imported plants that are drought-resistant in other climes and have successfully adapted to our own. We interviewed successful amateurs and seasoned professionals—each devoted to an informal laboratory—the garden.

Our readership grew slowly but surely. The Internet has become an effective way to provide low cost information to millions of readers—to have a personal relationship with those readers and act quickly, correct errors, and build archives of value. For a magazine, the Internet becomes an incubator. What do your readers choose? How can writers tailor their stories to readers' needs? Whether cooking fresh produce from the farmers markets or learning about growing culinary herbs, we were able to discover which stories were most popular. We followed those interests and continue to do so.

A few readers asked if we would consider collecting stories in book form. Computers, they suggested, were fine for working and researching, but not comfortable to curl up with on a cold winter night. Readers, they told us, like books, too. Now we have partnered with Fulcrum Publishing in Golden, who has guided us in the first of an extended series. We'll begin with guides to the Colorado outdoors, antiques, and homes and gardens, with more to come in the future. The old and new have conjoined. And whether you love the Internet, or prefer books, Front Range Living will give you the best of both worlds.

Paper or cyberspace—it still comes down to words and whether they engage, enlighten, or entertain us. New communications technologies alter those they push aside, but the old are remarkably resilient. The Internet won't do away with books. In fact, the two have become the newest of best friends. Front Range Living will provide an ongoing source of Colorado experiences for our readers. But when the day ends, and you want to slip under bedcovers with a cup of tea and a good book, we'll be available as a bedside companion, too.

—Niki Hayden, Editor

Front Range Living

It's hard to pin down exactly when ordinary America caught the fever to collect antiques. Perhaps some believed that antique collectors lived in crumbling New England homes packed with little-used old stuff. No more. Antiques are big business, sought out everywhere, and savored.

Maybe it starts with a dying relative who passes on a favorite collection. Uncle Dan gives up his mother's quilts; Aunt Mildred hands over her carefully preserved depression-era glassware. Heirs, who recognize that these items will never be made again, begin informal research. They flock to the Internet, various television programs on collecting, the neighborhood antiques dealer, or a museum to seek information. Along the way, a casual interest becomes a fascination. The most unlikely students end up as experts and mentors.

Collectors form a broad group of diverse individuals. Some are collecting the precious: silver, diamond jewelry, and rare European furniture. Others are devoted strictly to Americana: ceramics from the 1950s, toys of the twentieth century, Fiesta dinnerware from the 1930s. What they have in common is a love of history and a desire to care for their collections.

With such a vast array of collectibles to choose from, how do you get started? While there's no single avenue for everyone, here are a few well-beaten paths. Start with museums. The Denver Art Museum's decorative arts wing will share a history of furniture with you. Interested in collecting historical items of the pioneer past? Begin at the Colorado History Museum. Want to know more about quilts? Begin at the Rocky Mountain Quilt Museum in Golden. Get to know the Colorado Historical Society. At the same time, look in your hometown. Find the historical society of your city and get in touch with the staff. That's where you'll find invaluable sources.

If you want to collect books, seek out libraries that have rare book collections. Both the University of Colorado at Boulder and the Denver Public Library house antique books and have well-trained people to guide you.

Interested in something more recent, perhaps 1950s' jewelry? Seek out dealers who specialize in what you find fascinating. Roseville ceramics dealers, antique jewelry dealers, depression-glass dealers—these are individuals whose interests may not be represented in museums, but they have spent a lifetime getting to know their wares. Even if you're not ready to buy, they will happily share information with you. Dealers want their customers to be knowledgeable and savvy. You'll recognize reputable dealers when you see them—they have been in business for a long time. Other collectors will know them by name.

You'll find groups out there that band together for a common love of photography, quilting, woodworking, glassware, or architecture. Not all are devoted to antiques, but many investigate both historical and current trends in textiles, furniture, and architecture. Visit historic homes not only for ideas, but also for contacts and information. There's a sea of generous people who cherish historic homes and want to pass on their love of the past to others.

Attend antique shows, and always ask if they offer appraisals or classes. Even museums will often set aside several days each year for antique appraisals. For example, the Longmont Museum hosts appraisals on the first Saturday of October each year. You'll be able to get a ballpark sense of the worth of your special china or glassware, and you'll also pick up a considerable amount of information.

These days, the Internet looms large in antique buying and selling. The auction website www.ebay.com has made a fortune as a global market for antiques. It also serves as a price guide and can give you a rough approximation of what items may be selling for. But there are a few caveats about buying over the Internet. Buying quality items is important if you want to invest in antiques. "Always buy the best you can afford," is what established dealers will tell you. If you can't see and touch an item, you may not know what condition it is in. This is especially true for books, textiles, and other highly perishable collectibles.

When you buy an antique, it's chancy to believe that you've made an investment. What you have is an item that will face the vagaries of markets in the future. It may rise in value, but it may fall. The best example of this is silver, which once was a great investment, but fell in value as styles relaxed and people no longer wanted to polish elaborate silver flatware. Now it's resurging in popularity, despite our casual interiors. In fact, silver is stylish when mixed with more ordinary dinnerware, according to recent trends. But it has taken one or two generations to come to this realization.

Lastly, learn how to care for what you collect. Poor-quality antiques quickly turn into junk. Condition is paramount, not only for investing, but for preserving history. Dealers are particularly adept at helping you know how best to preserve that nineteenth-century woodblock print or early photograph. They've learned more about preservation of the perishable in the last ten years than was known in the last hundred.

Antiques now come from all over the world. Although Colorado does have a flavor of its own with western Americana and midwestern collectibles, you'll also find antiques from Tibet, South America, and India. Urban renewal in other countries means a fourteenth-century monastery door becomes twenty-first-century sculpture. Wars often unleash treasures when people flee their homes, and their prized objects, such as Oriental carpets, surface in the world markets. Antiques can be casualties of strife and often reveal a tragic and bloody story. These exotic finds reside side by side with twentieth-century American ceramics and sturdy turn-of-the-century oak furniture.

Whatever your interest, once you begin to collect, you'll step into a world of new friends, information, research, trips, and societies. In the end, you'll become one of those experts, too, who will be relied upon as a font of knowledge for aspiring collectors.

THE
PIONEER SPIRIT

■ Happy Trails: Western Memorabilia

by NIKI HAYDEN

As any Colorado history text will tell you, life in the pioneer West was dangerous, survival was hard-won, and supplies were often meager. How is it that out of this hardscrabble life grew one of the most colorful styles ever to be called American? Horse trappings braided and woven. Sturdy spurs punched with filigree. Leather saddles tattooed in florid swirls. Embroidered shirts, vividly dyed scarves, carved buckles, fancy-stitched boots—Hollywood may have stretched the limits of outrageous ornamentation, but the roots of flamboyance were always there.

The exaggerated portrait of cowboys in 1950s' movies can't explain the steady following of western style and taste. There's another factor to be considered. Colorado is studded with small horse farms—perhaps only three acres of house, barn, and corral in what could be called the last remnants of the old West. While cars and planes have revolutionized transportation, the romance of the horse lingers.

The romance of the horse lingers in the West.

Drive to northern Colorado, the home of saddlemaker Mark Howes, and you'll pass his corral of horses. One is lying on its back, wiggling with all legs in the air, to scratch an itch. "There's one old horse out there I really like," Mark says, with a nod to the three. Mark's Double H Ranch Saddles is a workshop dedicated to forging handmade saddles fit to order and as fancy as you wish. Like many westerners, Mark grew up with horses and learned to fix his own saddles at an early age. He managed ranches in Wyoming before returning to his Colorado home and setting up business. After twenty-five years, he's made a reputation for his saddlery in a craft that fits together horse and rider nearly perfectly.

At an auction in Mesa, Arizona, Roy Rogers' saddle, chaps, spurs, and horse regalia sold for $660,000. Western collectibles are big business. But Mark doesn't collect—not to sell, anyway. Just for old-times' sake. A few saddles are antiques to be lovingly restored. Others are polished and spiffy, like new shoes yet to be worn. "The horse industry is growing," Mark says to account for his backlog of business, "and people want the latest. Horses change, too, and that drives business. The trend has been the bulldog quarter horse, a strong, stiff-legged mover. Now I'm seeing more of the athletic thoroughbreds."

At the Double H Ranch in Fort Collins, Mark Howes makes saddles that fit horse to rider.

A Perfect Fit

Riders bring their horses to Mark, who measures them like a tailor would for a suit of clothes: "Horses' backs change. Sometimes their shoulders go up into their backs. You have to consider how old the horse is, how he will change in the future, how he will be used, and what the rider requirements are. First you fit the horse. Then you fit the rider."

Spurs and bits, both modern and old, are prized by collectors.

Mark's son is making spurs and bits—a part of the cowboy tradition that is collectible today both as antique and contemporary craft. Some, like Bill Adamson, are both historian and spur maker. Bill's dad, in his early days, had been a cowboy. "He didn't talk much about it," Bill says, "but when he did, I sure listened." He studies the earlier spur makers like Oscar Crockett, who moved from Texas to Boulder, Colorado. Although Oscar died in 1949, his company survived from 1920 to 1984. "The

Crocketts were the only spur makers who had a cowboy background," Bill says. "They just had the credentials, combined with hard work and showmanship."

Ask Bill about the collecting world today, and he'll hand you some warnings. There's fraud out there for the unprepared. He's seen one antique spur matched with another of duplicate reconstruction: "The most common fraud is representing new goods as older goods. It's all the way from an artfully crafted description to accelerated aging and applying a fraudulent mark." But he believes younger collectors coming into the business are wise to these ploys.

American saddles in the West reveal a Spanish influence.

"Today there are books out that show the proper spurs," he says. Books didn't exist when he first chanced upon old spurs. Go to shows and talk to the old dealers. Find the experts. Get reprints of catalogs that will detail the looks and prices of western antiques. That's his advice. As with most antiques, he says, "The value of quality goes up, while the mediocre and poor go down."

Or, buy contemporary. American spur makers are dabbling in elaborate and beautifully made horse regalia. Most of the ordinary spurs now come from China, so American spur makers have drifted toward the one-of-a-kind collectible pieces, which Bill calls "fabulously high-end stuff."

A World History

Spurs, like saddles, carry a history wider than the American West. You'll find saddles all over the world, with each culture trying to fit a rider onto a horse. A Chinese saddle, Mark points out, is upright and formal with the look of a chair.

Take a close look at old American saddles, and you may notice a Spanish influence. Mexican cowboys drove cattle across the Tex–Mex border, bringing

Braids and coils are a few of the flamboyant horse trappings of the West.

chaps and spurs, broad-brimmed hats, and ornate leatherwork. Cowboys added jeans, plaids, and vests, and the two styles blended, much like border food today.

"Earlier than that was the Moorish influence in Spain," Mark says, as he leafs through a book on the history of saddle making. Moorish markings are heavily stylized according to Muslim influence, which made all living creatures melt into abstraction. That intricate detail later transferred to the Spanish designs.

If the line demarcating Mexican West and American West was fuzzy from the beginning, it's still fuzzy today. "I love it when the Mexican and cowboy designs blend," says Bets Hannah, children's clothing designer and avid collector. She and her husband, Jim, have scoured thrift shops for fifteen years in search of western design. Ties, wooden platters, books, fabric, pottery, calendars, posters, shirts, boots, felt jackets—most from the 1940s and 1950s—all are grist for design ideas.

Mexicali

Bets owned a horse as a young girl, but it hardly matters that she doesn't now. The vintage clothing, tablecloths, and beer trays from Mexico center around the familiar icons: bucking broncos, señoritas, Conestoga wagons, sleeping sombrero guys poised as salt-and-pepper shakers. It's a blend that Bets calls Mexicali, but the familiarity is as American as Roy Rogers and Dale Evans.

Salt-and-pepper shakers of two sombrero guys were popular in the 1950s.

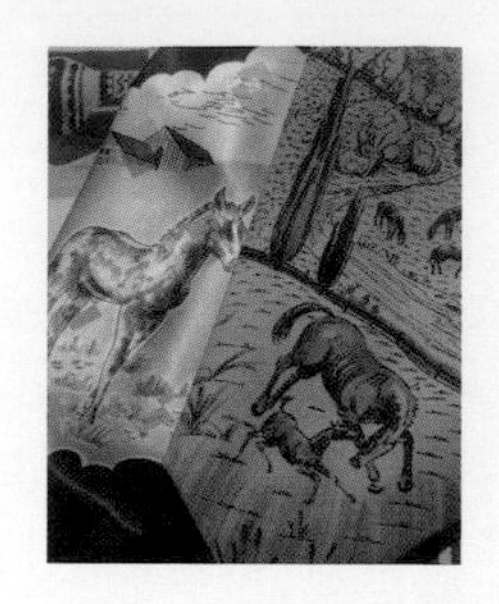

"We've just picked up everything for a dollar here, a few there. I'm glad that our collection isn't valuable," she says, although that may change. American West style remains popular, but the ordinary, everyday western accessories have been so loved and used that little remains. Jim still haunts thrift shops looking for silk ties with horse heads and broncos, but they're less commonly chanced upon now.

Instead, Bets looks for Mexican calendar art from the 1940s, when artists rendered señoritas and their handsome companions alongside guitars and beautiful horses. Dolores del Rio, the Hollywood actress who so often portrayed a señorita, smiles in one portrait. Colorful beer trays almost always convey a beautiful Mexican woman in white puckered peasant blouse with a tiered, full skirt and glinting silver jewelry. But you'll rarely find their charming prints today. "What you see is just the logo of the beer or soft drink," Bets says.

Mexican calendar art is colorful, dramatic, and affordable.

Painted wooden trays line a wall in her home. Flowers in florid strokes echo vibrant Mexican embroidery. Woven trays surround calendar art, which has been clipped and framed behind glass. Homer Laughlin, makers of Fiestaware in West Virginia, also manufactured a line of Mexican-motif pottery. Rustic brown pottery from Tlaquepaque lines up on shelves. Silk screen portraits of cacti, horses, and ranch scenes parade on a soft white background of cotton towels. Conestoga wagons, pulled by

Felted clothing is studded with embroidery, creating a tapestry of textures and colors. Platters are hand-painted with expressive strokes. It's all a part of folk art from the Border that evoked a Western romance.

sweating teams of horses, careen across red curtains. Tiny western boots, creased and cracked, line up alongside childhood photos of Jim and Bets, dressed in toddler cowboy hats and fringed shirts—western fans from the cradle.

There's not a single image of a gun or animal cruelty in the Hannah house, or in the children's clothes she designs. They're not necessary for her imagination. The West, she points out, was rich in bold colors at a time when traditional American colors were subdued. Western scenes were dramatic, which she demonstrates by pointing to the silhouettes of black stallions rearing against a red sky. Perhaps it was the majestic landscape or the colorful assortment of people, the extravagant costumes and pageantry. Whatever the inspiration, "The West was a wonderful romance," she says. In a style that is recognized all over the world, those familiar images remain with us still.

RESOURCES

■ SHOPS AND DEALERS

ARVADA

Territorial Trade, 5752 Olde Wadsworth Boulevard, 80002; 303-463-8131; www.territorialtrader.com. Western clothing is carried.

DENVER

Cry Baby Ranch, 1422 Larimer Street, 80202; 303-623-3979; www.crybabyranch.com. Large selection of western collectibles, clothing, home decor; Bets Hannah's clothing line, Gaucho, is carried.

David Cook Fine American Art, 1637 Wazee Street, 80202; 303-623-8181; www.davidcookfineamericanart.com. Southwestern rugs, especially historic Navajo.

Gallagher Collection, 1298 South Broadway, 80210; in the Antique Guild; 303-756-5821. Books only.

Lewis Bobrick Antiques, 1213 East Fourth Avenue, 80218; 303-744-9203; www.lewisbobrickantiques.com. Southwestern rugs.

Native American Trading Company, 1301 Bannock Street, 80204; 303-534-0771; www.nativeamericantradingco.com.

LONGMONT AND LYONS

Cowboy Classics; 303-776-7142; www.t-m-cowboyclassics.com. Tom and Maril Bice make and sell western furniture from their home in Longmont, and sell over the Internet.

Left-Hand Trading Company, 401 Main Street, Lyons, 80540; 303-823-0743, www.lefthandtrading company.com. Western room filled with antique furniture, accessories, books, jewelry of the West.

MANITOU SPRINGS

Ruxton's Trading Post, 22 Ruxton Avenue, 80829; 719-635-0588; www.oldwestantiques.com. Wide range of western items; also information on the Pikes Peak Western Show.

Western Shop, 807 Manitou Avenue, 80829; 719-685-5026. Western clothing.

MOUNTAIN COMMUNITIES

Antique Accents, 155 Main Street, Minturn, 81645; 970-827-9070. Antiques and memorabilia.

Crystal Farm, 18 Antelope Road, Redstone, 81623; 970-963-2350; www.crystalfarm.com. Antler furniture and lighting.

Jerry Becker, 200 Aspen Lane, Pine, 80470; 303-838-6245, by appointment only. Antique Navajo rugs and textiles from the Southwest.

Kemo Sabe, 434 East Cooper Avenue, Aspen, 81611; 970-925-7878. Western hats, boots, home furnishings.

Oil City Merchants, 126 West Main Street, Florence, 81226; 719-784-6582. Western antiques.

The Sandman, Inc., and Buckskin Booksellers, 505 Main Street, Suite 110, Beaumont Hotel, Ouray, 81427; 970-325-4044. Memorabilia, new and used books.

Telluride Antique Market, 324 West Colorado Avenue, Telluride, 81435; 970-728-4323. Western memorabilia.

■ COLLECTIBLES SHOWS

Bit & Spur Auction, Larimer County Fairgrounds, Loveland; 970-669-6760. Usually held mid-June.

Pikes Peak Western Show: *see* Ruxton's Trading Post under Manitou Springs; www.oldwestantiques.com.

■ FLEA MARKETS

Ballpark Flea Market, outdoors at Twenty-second and Larimer Streets, Denver; www.ballparkmarket.com.

■ MUSEUMS

Buffalo Bill Cody Memorial Museum and Grave, 987-½ Lookout Mountain Road, Golden, 80401; 303-526-0747; www.buffalobill.org.

Colorado History Museum, 1300 Broadway, Denver, 80203; 303-866-3681; www.coloradohistory.org.

Colorado Springs Fine Arts Center, 30 West Dale Street, Colorado Springs, 80903; 719-634-5581; www.csfineartscenter.org. Hispanic and Pueblo collections as well as traditional western art.

Hiwan Homestead Museum, 4208 South Timbervale Drive, Evergreen, 80439; 303-674-6262; http://co.jefferson.co.us. Nineteenth-century log home furnished in the style of the 1920s and 1930s.

Baca House, Bloom Mansion, and Pioneer Museum, 300 East Main Street, Trinidad, 81082; 719-846-7217; www.coloradohistory.org.

Pro Rodeo Hall of Fame, 101 Pro Rodeo Drive, Colorado Springs, 80919; 719-593-8840; www.prorodeo.com.

■ SADDLE MAKER

Double H Ranch Saddle Shop, Mark Howes, Fort Collins; 970-482-6229.

■ RECOMMENDED READING

Cowboys & Indians magazine; 800-982-5370; www.cowboysindians.com.

American Cowboy magazine, P.O. Box 6630, Sheridan, Wyoming 82801; 307-672-7171; www.americancowboy.com.

Quilts: Soft Quilts, Strong Stories

by DIANNE ZUCKERMAN AND NIKI HAYDEN

From pioneer women's patchwork legacies to the AIDS Memorial Quilt, unfurled over grassy acres like an endless field of flowers, soft quilts tell strong stories.

The simplest of quilts, handed down over time and faded from years of use, might have warmed a western settler's bed or kept cold winds from seeping through cracks in a cabin wall. More elaborate patterns speak of a longing for beauty and artistic expression or tout causes such as patriotic celebrations and civil rights.

Quilts have covered every aspect of daily life, from welcoming newborns to comforting the old and dying. Often passed down from one generation to the next, quilts can serve as a kind of fabric family album, a memory bank of individuals and events that shaped people's lives and histories. To a large extent, those histories are American.

Timeworn quilts retain a love for texture, color, simplicity and comfort.

Patchwork: Uniquely American

"Quilting itself isn't strictly American," says Alisa S. Zahller, assistant curator of decorative and fine arts at the Colorado History Museum in Denver. "Women who came to America brought with them certain traditions—there are garments that were quilted in medieval times. But patchwork quilts and piecework quilts really are uniquely an American style."

Quilting was part of the fabric of American life as far back as colonial times. But patchwork quilts particularly recall hardy nineteenth-century pioneer women who recycled worn textiles into creative designs to compensate for a paucity of new bolts of cloth.

Even in the bleakest of times, women created elaborate quilts with delicate stitches. This Broken Star quilt is by Pearl Metsker.

For emigrant families who had endured the harsh journey across open prairie in a rough wagon, living in a cabin, no matter how simple, must have been a welcome alternative. This sense of home and hearth is at the heart of the Log Cabin quilt, which incorporates a central "chimney" block surrounded by varicolored strips or "logs."

Western Sentiments

The Colorado History Museum's collection, which features striking traditional and contemporary quilts crafted by Colorado residents, includes a Log Cabin quilt made in 1885. Warm and earthy, with overlapping light and dark sections, the coverlet has a solid, orderly feel. It was made by seventeen-year-old Nellie Jean Nichols, who may have been anticipating her future marriage and the opportunity to establish her own home fires.

Another type of quilt that became popular around the same time, during a period of sentimentality and separation as people headed west, was friendship, or album, quilts. One variation on this was the autograph quilt, inspired by the era's popular leather-bound inscription books. While autograph quilts usually involved stitching together fabric sections featuring signatures of family and friends, a nineteenth-century woman named Emma Schoefield Wright took a somewhat different approach.

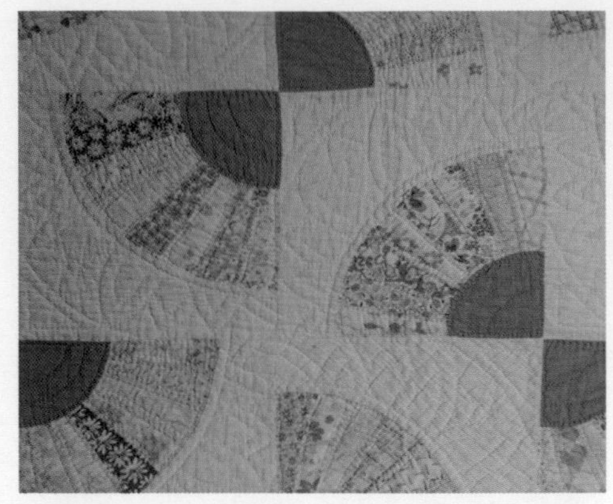

The Fan quilt, all in pastels, displays snippets of dress fabrics from long ago.

Her 1880 autograph quilt includes pieced geometric blocks signed by notables of the period. Wright, an established painter, created graceful illustrations of flowers and waterfalls to set off the signatures of Ulysses S. Grant, the Archbishop of Canterbury, and other luminaries. In addition to being a kind of "Who's Who" of the time, the caliber of the signatures also says something about the status of Wright and her father, an early president of the Burlington Northern Railroad.

While Emma's father helped her collect autographs, quilts more often represented collaborations between daughters and their mothers or grandmothers. In the nineteenth century, girls usually began learning to quilt by the time they were about eight years old. After extensive practice, they were ready to embark upon their own doll-size efforts.

A Social Gathering

While there are numerous examples of stunning quilts made to recognize individuals, perhaps the overriding theme in quilting is the role it has always played in bringing together members of a community. In the nineteenth century, quilting was one of the few social pastimes available to women—particularly those who lived in sparsely settled western towns.

As the women gathered to sew and socialize, their needlework creations often evolved into charitable works, sold to raise money for a church, hospital, or other community institution. In addition to displaying the group's creative flair, quilting bees also became synonymous with women coming together for support and shared experiences.

Among the quilts in the Colorado History Museum is the Colorado Japanese American Women's Quilt Project, which presents the experiences of women of Japanese ancestry living in the United States, particularly Colorado. Created in 1995, the panels of patchwork squares integrate scenes and symbols of both Japan and Colorado.

A pair of traditional good-fortune cranes, gold wings bending gracefully against a flowered backdrop, are mounted only a glimpse away from darker remembrances, such as a group of Japanese people being forcibly moved to the Amache Relocation Center in Granada, Colorado, during World War II.

Such images embody both the best hopes and worst events in people's lives. Together, they sum up much of what quilting has come to represent. For the maker, it's a way of giving voice to life's important moments. For later viewers, it's a way to identify with those who came before.

The Double Wedding Ring quilt was pieced by Bertha Landaker, one of the first members of the Last Chance quilters.

For Alisa, exhibits are an opportunity to link individuals and eras. "The thing I hope people consider is that it makes them reminisce, makes them think about objects in a new way, helps them learn about Colorado's history and different places. I hope it's a personal connection that they're able to make with the artifacts and the stories."

The Ladies of Last Chance

On U.S. Highway 36, midway between Denver and Kansas, sits the town of Last Chance. Once, it was the last stop for gas, food, or water before setting off on a long drive east or west. Today, you'll find a Dairy King and a Methodist Church. While you can stop for a sundae or a prayer in Last Chance, you won't find gas, lodging, or groceries.

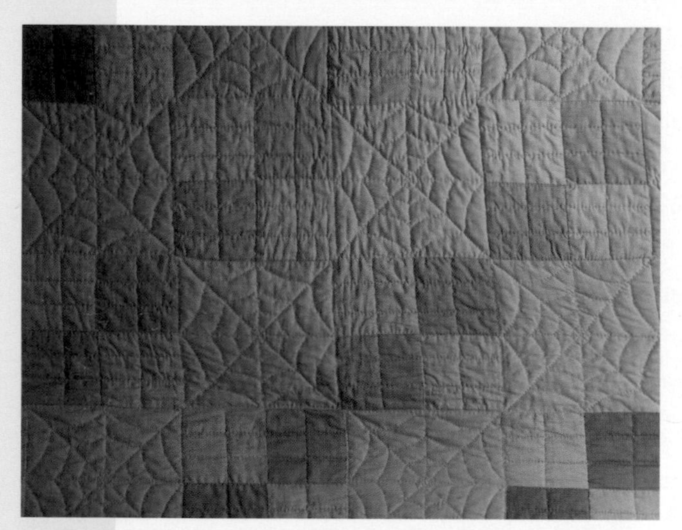

Even the simplest block forms are stunning in rich colors. Called Four Patch, this quilt was pieced by Lydia Chenoweth.

The dwindling farm population has made small towns in eastern Colorado smaller. If you're stranded in Last Chance, a generous farm family keeps gas available, but there's no station for miles around. Surprisingly, after years of a continuing exodus, one tiny community has stayed put. The Last Chance quilters, who banded together in 1926, are reckoned to be the oldest continuous quilting group in Colorado. Once a week, as few as four, and as many as twelve, arrive. Potluck fare—from macaroni and cheese to salads and dessert—line up, poised for lunch. Ranging in age from twenty-three to more than ninety, the Last Chance ladies huddle around a stretched quilt.

Several members are second and third generation from the same family. Opal Roderick's two daughters and a granddaughter might show up. "My mother was not a quilter," she says, "but my mother-in-law was. She came from Tennessee and helped me with my first quilt." Opal joined the group in 1955 when her first child was born. At that time, the Last Chance ladies quilted in each other's homes, rolling up the quilts, packing them in a car with half the quilt sticking out a car window. But when the brick Methodist Church was built on the original site of a sod house, quilting regularly began in earnest.

A Prized Object Made from Scraps

Quilting may be fashionable today, but originally it was a clever way to recycle fabric scraps—and for some, still is. "Why, some of these old quilts, they sewed two tiny pieces of fabric together to make another tiny piece," Elsie Hood says. "That's how they saved. So often, you saved the tails of men's shirts. The elbows might wear out in a man's shirts, but the tails were good, not bleached by the sun." All went into a scrap bag.

Elsie still insists on using scraps for her quilts. She's partial to pastels and remembers recycling flour sacks, even feed sacks. The prints were prettier back then and the fabric soft. Friends traded scraps to get a rainbow of colors. Darning socks was a night's pastime, and Elsie made most of her children's clothes. Now that she's over ninety, Elsie has a quilting frame set up in the living room, dragged up from the basement. The living room is sunny, warm, and well lit, she notes, although the frame takes up most of the space.

Johnny Round the Clock, made by Claudia Luna with hand-dyed fabric and carded cotton batting, dates to 1882.

"I really learned quilting at Last Chance," she says, "although my mother-in-law made a quilt for me when I married. She had two sons, and

Sunbonnet Sue was a favorite quilt for little girls. Dress fabrics will reveal the approximate time the quilt was made—in this case the 1930s.

my sister married her other son. Mine was a Bow-Tie quilt. My mom would take the wool off the sheep, then wash it quite a bit and dry it on the roof in the sun. She carded it in a long strip, laid it on her flannel cloth, and then simply tied it to keep it together. Houses back then were not heated at night. And you didn't have warm clothing like the down jackets we have today. Back then you got by on less. It was a different lifestyle and didn't take as much cash."

Audrey Gilchrist joined the group in 1945, just a year or two after she was married at the age of sixteen. "When I was making things to be married, my dad gave me one hundred dollars out of the bean crop for my wedding. I used cotton batting then. Some people used wool if they had that. I ordered from Montgomery Ward or Sears and Roebuck. Little country stores didn't keep much in the way of materials. But most fabrics were pieces, scraps, what you had from making clothes."

The Last Chance ladies quilt for others. Often they are handed antique quilts, family heirlooms that never were completed. The tops, inside batting, and quilt bottoms are sandwiched together. They quilt the three layers and charge a fee, which goes to maintain the church. And while many are church members, the group also includes Roman Catholics and members of the Church of Jesus Christ of Latter-day Saints. "It always was nondenominational," Elsie says—anyone is welcome to potluck and quilt.

Each Quilt Tells a Story

At the Rocky Mountain Quilt Museum in Golden, the ladies from Last Chance display an array of quilts. They have pieced, appliquéd, and quilted most of the displayed quilts. But some are collected from old friends or family. Each tells a story. One includes the tiny stitches and pieced work of a four-year-old child. She was Opal's mother. Audrey has brought the quilt of Bertha Landaker, one of the original members of the Last Chance ladies. The Double Wedding Ring is a favorite pattern, and Bertha was a treasured friend. Other quilts celebrate a wedding, a newborn, or memories handed down in the family. They're whimsical, autobiographical, practical, and artistic. One, called Sunbonnet Sue, is pieced from dresses of the 1930s. It's obviously a quilt for a little girl, with a parade of tiny dolls, each sporting a bonnet, marching in rows.

Every quilt marks a month or more of work, a few nearly a lifetime of effort, as each woman watched the years roll by. Marriages, births, deaths, and neighbors moving away—those stories are told in the quilts. The hours spent together are another way of sharing stories. "Why, if I don't go, I feel like I'm sick," Elsie says. "You catch up on the news and the happenings."

Elsie loves pastels and tiny, pieced work expertly quilted by hand. But the machines that quilt quickly are just as good, she believes. And techniques of layering and cutting fabric are time-savers. The availability of synthetic fibers is a welcome addition to many. "I prefer a blend in fabrics," Opal says. "Cotton is awfully hard to get so it doesn't wrinkle. And I prefer to piece on the machine."

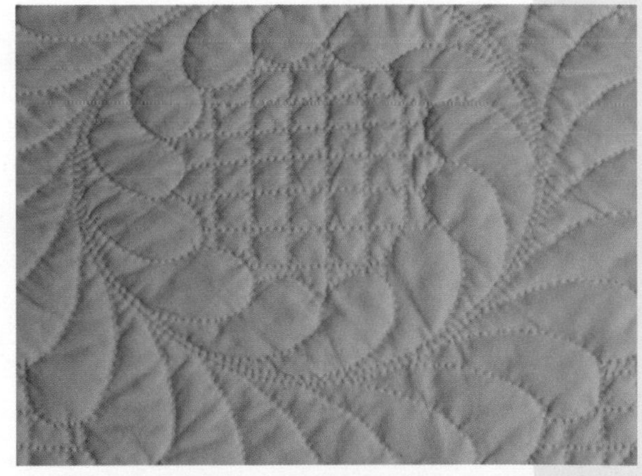

Fine stitching is the hallmark of expert quilting.

Quilting a Continuity in the Midst of Change

Like other members, Opal came from a farming family. Cattle and wheat are the main crops around Last Chance, she says, but farming is on the wane. Grown children have left the region. Elsie's farm is empty, so is her sister's, and a neighbor's to the south, too. Farms have grown bigger but need fewer workers. "We started with horses first and later got a tractor. The farmers went to bigger machinery and more land. We didn't use machinery like they do today."

Audrey has seen huge sweeps of land taken over to consolidate the agriculture industry. "There's no room for the little guy today," she says. In contrast, quilting is a shared, timeless experience despite swirling changes. The continuity is comforting.

These women miss the cluster of small farms that dotted their landscape. But they don't miss some of the harsh times from the past. As bad as a recent drought has been for Colorado, Elsie remembers worse. "In thirty-three and fifty-five," she recalls, and Audrey adds that they didn't have irrigation wells back then. "We had terrible dirt storms in the thirties. You couldn't see across the street. Thousands of little whirlwinds all came together. You'd better have your hand on the doorknob when that happened."

RESOURCES

MUSEUMS

Colorado History Museum, 1300 Broadway, Denver, 80203; 303-866-3682; www.coloradohistory.org/hist_sites/CHM/Colorado_History_Museum.htm.

Denver Art Museum, 100 West 14th Avenue, Denver, 80204; 720-865-5000;www.denverartmuseum.org. Good collection of nineteenth- and early twentieth-century Colorado quilts.

Front Range Quilters; www.artquilters.org. A group of contemporary quilters.

Rocky Mountain Quilt Museum, 1111 Washington Avenue, Golden, 80401; 303-277-0377; www.rmqm.org. Quilt collection and information about caring for antique quilts.

RECOMMENDED READING

The American Quilt: A History of Cloth and Comfort 1750–1950 by Roderick Kiracofe and Mary Elizabeth Johnson (Clarkson N. Potter, 1993). Provides more information about the history of quilts and their makers.

■ Snapshots in Time: Collecting and Preserving Antique Photos

by NIKI HAYDEN

Chief Wolf Robe from the Southern Cheyenne sits for a portrait in Washington, D.C., June 1909. Light has fallen on his face and shoulders, and through a nineteenth-century discovery called photography, his presence is captured. Nearly one hundred years later, we are transported as onlookers to that location and a remarkable moment in our history.

Chief Wolf Robe was photographed by De Lancey W. Gill in 1909.

As a witness to tragedy, photography arrived in America to chronicle a profound event: the Civil War. Photography documented horrifying images, which revealed scenes that no artist could blunt with a romanticized brush stroke. The shock inspired an entire generation, traumatized and saddened, to seek stories beyond the battlefields. So when the federal government sent survey teams out west, they included photographers charged with preserving a more uplifting tale: a breathtaking landscape unsullied and ready to plow, wilderness brimming with game and timber, caves hinting at silver, rivers glinting with gold.

Photography marked the opening of the American West and coincided with Colorado's complex history. And while there is always a story in a photo, truth proved to be elusive—from the very beginning.

"William Henry Jackson was sent out with the Hayden Survey," says Colorado historical photo collector Rob Lewis, "and Timothy O'Sullivan was sent on two surveys. Jackson would take photos of snow and waterfalls so settlers would know there was water. O'Sullivan would record bleak landscapes that would not entice. O'Sullivan had his own aesthetic. That's why I think people today hold him in great esteem," Rob says.

Ironically, photographers unwittingly left us a history that documents plunder: "A beautiful landscape becomes scarred. When you see tunnels blasted, trees felled, mining operations denuding the forests, from one point of view that is progress. But, from a contemporary aesthetic, there are so few places that are left. Our environment is fragile. We have destroyed habitat and ecosystems," Rob says.

Frank Jay Haynes captured the Grand Canyon of the Yellowstone and Falls, Dakota Territory, 1882.

Photos hail a bustling silver mining town that, just a few years later, is abandoned. Mines are etched into the earth only to become quickly depleted. "People flooded in, built their houses where they could, stripped the resources, and left," he says.

Back east, mired in postwar scandals and misery, the West held out a promise of better days. There was plenty about the American West to draw settlers if they could be assured of fertile land and security. While skeptical easterners believed the West to be a great desert populated by fierce people, politicians and railroad magnates urged photographers to send back images of a bountiful land with Indians signing peace treaties. Photos tell a story.

Cultural Clash

"Any time you see a photo of a Native American, isn't it already too late for their culture? In order to feel comfortable for a photographer to march up to an Indian, there was a threat of force," Rob says. A thread of truth is revealed in a progression of photographs: the early survey photos of Indians with guns and knives, then the delegation of Native American leaders seated on Victorian chairs, signing away their land. The reservation and massacre photos, tragic and haunting, complete the picture.

Geronimo with his son and braves was photographed by C.S. Fly.

By the early twentieth century, a different Native American looks into the camera—noble, romanticized, dressed up by Edward Curtis. "After the turn of the century, I can hardly stomach those saccharine pictures of Indians re-created by our culture. You don't see the alcoholism, disease, illiteracy," Rob says.

Zealous Adventurers

Rob collects photos dating from 1857 to about 1900, the years that defined the western frontier. Photography was a new technology, one that required skill and perseverance. "In learning about the history of the photos, I learn about the history of the medium. What was going on then was the equivalent of the digital age, of the Internet," he says.

John Hillers reveals a daunting landscape in the Grand To-Wip Valley.

Photography was difficult at best, requiring zealous adventurers to climb mountains, assisted by mules burdened under heavy loads of glass plates and dangerous chemicals. "Everything from setting up your negative and getting plates back to the studio with a direct contact plate, to solar printed by direct sunlight—these early photographers had to be passionate and knowledgeable in order to come up with wonderful images," Rob says. And while we take photography for granted today, knowing how perilous many of these treks could be makes historical photos all the more remarkable.

Nighthawk in his nest dates to 1885–1890 by L. A. Huffman.

Old Photos Endure

In the last 150 years, photos have varied in durability. Most black-and-white photos taken before and just after 1900 are more stable than later photos, and certainly more so than early color photography. Judy Steiner, associate curator of photography at the Colorado Historical Society, says that early color photography has to be kept in a freezer to conserve the images. Early black-and-white, in contrast, often was printed on a paper of superior quality and used excellent chemicals that have survived the test of time.

The Historical Society holds a remarkable collection by William Henry Jackson from the Hayden Survey. "The strength of our collection is late nineteenth and early twentieth century," Judy says. Another of those collections within their holdings is the Aultman Studio, which was operated by father and sons for nearly one hundred years in Trinidad, Colorado, taking 40,000 photos. Unlike the landscape photos of Jackson, the Aultmans photographed families—Hispanic, African American, and Anglo. They covered the Santa Fe Trail travelers, coal miners, ranchers, and train workers. It's a particularly valuable collection because most early studios discarded photo negatives or sold glass plates to greenhouses.

Collecting Photos

"Photography is transient," Judy says with a sigh, "and relatively recent compared to prints and paintings." Only in the last few decades have photos been granted a status prompting serious collecting. For collectors like Rob, finding photos often stems from what he calls "the three Ds—death, divorce, and debt." He haunts auctions, galleries, and existing collections. Rob has even sold photos only to buy them back later. "The difference between a dealer and a collector is just a matter of time," he quips. Although the biggest money is in early twentieth-century masters, Rob is drawn to the stark, heart-rending images of earlier days.

Andrew Frank and his wife pose for C. C. McBride.

Photo books may instruct you to buy an image from each famous twentieth-century master, but Rob disagrees. He calls that "collecting by number." Collect what you love and make a statement of your own, he says. And for new, young collectors, contemporary photographers are worth collecting, prizing, and archiving. "There's no way to get an education first and buy secondly. You must pay for your education; you have to put your money out there and make mistakes. Go to exhibitions. Go to dealers. Many dealers are willing to talk to you. Talk to librarians. Hold the material and look at one print against another. When you start looking at it day after day, you discover your aesthetic. Find out what interests you and pursue it with passion. And always buy the finest quality, not the deals. Lesser quality will flounder in the market," he says.

C. C. McBride photographed a group simply described as "Ute agitators."

Choice photos, like fine prints and linens, require care to preserve that high quality. Light and humidity will destroy their value. If you frame your photos, make sure to employ a framer who understands the archival needs of preserving photography. Keep photos in a dry, dark place. Separate any negatives you may have from the prints, and don't store them in the attic or basement. Both places have wide fluctuations in temperature, which will degrade photos. Judy says that the Historical Society will answer questions on photo conservation over the phone. And while they are not paper conservators, they have experts who can direct callers to the appropriate resources.

If you'd like to collect photos, or simply research the photographic history of Colorado, begin at your public library. From there, move on to the public holdings of the Denver Public Library and, eventually, their Western History Room. The library also contains many digitized photos that are available on their website.

The Historical Society, which is located in the Colorado History Museum, offers a noncirculating library rich in resources.

Looking at photos is a lifelong endeavor, and one that you may want to share. Most collectors eventually lend their holdings to public institutions. Rob has sent his collection to the Smithsonian's Corcoran Gallery in Washington, D.C. "Certain images speak to anyone," he says, for photography is the most democratic of all art forms. "To find a great image in great condition with wonderful provenance—the creative instant of the artist and yourself—it's difficult to obtain. But like reaching perfection, you strive for it."

(All photos courtesy of the Robert G. Lewis Collection.)

RESOURCES

■ ORGANIZATIONS

Photographic Historical Society, P.O. Box 39563, Rochester, New York 14604; www.rit.edu/~andpph/tphs.html.

Denver Public Library, 10 West Fourteenth Avenue, Denver, 80204; 720-865-1111; www.denver.lib.co.us.

Association of International Photography Art Dealers, 1609 Connecticut Avenue NW, Washington, D.C. 20009; 202-986-0105; www.artline.com/associations/ipa/ipa.html.

Colorado Historical Society, 1300 Broadway, Denver, 80203; 303-866-3682; www.coloradohistory.org.

Daguerreian Society, 3043 West Liberty Avenue, Suite 9, Dormont, Pennsylvania 15216; 412-343-5525; www.daguerre.org.

Denver Posse of the Westerners; www.westerners-intl.org. Western history enthusiasts.

Light Impressions, P.O. Box 787, Brea, California 92822; 800-828-6216; www.lightimpressionsdirect.com. Provides archival supplies for photos.

National Stereoscopic Organization, P.O. Box 14801, Columbus, Ohio 43214.

A Genteel Age

Jewelry: Antique Rings for Modern Couples

by CAROL WARD

In the past, engaged women and their fiancés preferred to purchase and perhaps design a ring symbolic of a new beginning. Usually it was a diamond, the symbol for infinity. While today's couples are looking forward to the future, they're looking to the past for their engagement and wedding rings. Whether Victorian, Edwardian, or art deco, the question asked in many jewelry and antique shops is: "Where are your antique rings?"

The swing toward antique pieces of jewelry and stones other than diamonds may have developed in the 1980s when Prince Charles presented Diana, the late princess of Wales, with a sapphire and diamond engagement ring. American women noticed.

A 1910 Edwardian kite-shaped ring has a center mine-cut diamond surrounded by smaller diamonds.

"Women also notice what the movie stars are wearing," says antiques dealer Diane Bedell. "Hollywood stars are wearing antique and vintage jewelry a lot these days." As always, the fashion industry has immeasurable influence. In *Vogue* magazine a model is wearing two Victorian bracelets, Diane notes.

Antique rings offer an array of stones, including precious—sapphires, emeralds, and rubies—and many semiprecious stones, coupled with lovely filigree settings and exceptional expertise.

"Another wonderful aspect of antique rings is that the stone is set to appear larger," Diane says. "You get more bang for your buck." Craftspeople may have had to work harder to enhance the ring because cutting methods weren't as sophisticated as they are today. The way a diamond is cut is one of the clues to the age of the piece.

The top ring is a mine-cut ruby and diamond, 1915. The bottom ring is a traditional engagement ring from the 1930s.

Typical Early Cuts for Diamonds

In a table-cut diamond, the point of the stone is polished off, leaving the surface flat, like a tabletop. A sixteenth-century cut, the rose cut, has a flat base with facets branching out from the center of the stone in multiples of six, which create a rosebud opening. The old-mine cut was an earlier version of the modern round. This cut has a square shape, the crown is high, and the table (top of the stone) is small. And the European cut, which occurred in the mid-1800s, is similar to the old-mine cut but round rather than square, with 58 facets. The crown is higher than modern cuts, but not as high as the old-mine cut.

Some of these older cuts may have inclusions (flaws in the stone) and can be dull and lifeless. Others are near-perfect stones with lots of fire. A buyer today must weigh the inclusion and possible lower brilliance of the stone against what the ring does offer: beauty, detail, uniqueness, and a lower price tag.

An antique ring—diamond or other stones—costs a lot less money than today's new rings. "The industry is pushing 'white' [colorless] diamonds," says Diane. "A new ring will cost a great deal more."

"Everyone gets a De Beers," says jewelry collector Rei Elliott of Farmington, Massachusetts, a visitor to Colorado and avid antique shopper. "There's no individuality, everyone's a copycat. Break away from that mentality." Elliott cites the sapphire as her ring of choice. "That's what the ancient Egyptian kings and queens wore." After diamonds, antique sapphires sell best as engagement rings, Diane says.

Going back to the early nineteenth century, in the Georgian period, you'll find the cluster ring, which contains a cluster of perhaps small pearls and Persian turquoise surrounding a stone such as a red garnet in a setting of delicate scrollwork.

Queen Victoria ruled for sixty-four years, and she loved jewelry. Her long reign greatly influenced not just people in Britain but in Europe and the United States as well. There was her popular snake ring, hair jewelry (jewelry made out of strands of hair), and her "mourning" jet (black) jewelry, which she wore after her husband, Prince Albert, died. She was especially fond of wearing sentimental jewelry; for example, a ring set with gems interspersed in a band of clasped hands or gems spelling out the word *regard* on a ring band.

The top ring is art deco, 1920. The bottom diamond ring dates to 1900.

But, by the end of the century, designers and jewelers of the arts and crafts and art nouveau movements opposed the mass production and fanciful jewels in favor of simpler, individualistic designs. Styles followed the art nouveau forms of organic, flowery, naturalistic shapes. Rings were silver or gold set with pearls, opals, moonstones, or enameling. Platinum was discovered in the late 1800s. A harder metal than gold or silver but silver in color, platinum lent itself to numerous designs in antique jewelry.

In the early twentieth century, the Edwardian period returned to gems. One of the most distinctive aspects of Edwardian rings is the French-influenced delicate and lacy design. Amethysts, blue sapphires, green garnets, rubies, opals, and turquoise combine with diamonds and pearls. Bows, garlands, and swags in the rococo revival style are classic ornamentations on bands and gem settings.

An aquamarine stone is set among diamonds.

Diamonds and platinum continued into the 1920s, but designs changed dramatically with the introduction of the abstract art deco style. Geometric forms and unusual cuts included aquamarine, topaz, and citrine, which accommodated the demand for bigger gems and semiprecious stones. French jewelers Cartier and Boucheron dominated Europe, while Tiffany emerged as the leading jeweler of the United States.

Four Cs vs. Three Cs

While the four Cs—color, clarity, cut, and carat—are the relevant factors for buying diamonds, for colored stones there are the three Cs—color, color, and color. In the color arena be concerned with the following:

Hue—The precise color of the spectrum—red, orange, yellow, green, blue, violet, and indigo.

Intensity—Is the color bright and vivid? Or, is it dull and drab?

Tone—How much black, white, gray, or brown is present? Basically—how light or dark is the stone?

Distribution—Is the color evenly distributed throughout the stone?

There is a multitude of colors and shades, but look for a stone that is not drab, dull, or dirty. Some people like to choose a color based on their birth month or a symbolic trait important to them. The origin of the belief that a special stone was dedicated to each month and possesses a special virtue goes back to the first century A.D.

The following list of birthstones for months of the year was determined in 1912 by the American National Association of Jewelers:

January—Garnet	May—Emerald	September—Sapphire
February—Amethyst	June—Pearl	October—Opal
March—Bloodstone	July—Ruby	November—Topaz
April—Diamond	August—Peridot	December—Turquoise

Guessing at the meanings of stones can be fun, although we may never know exactly when or why a particular stone is symbolic. Did you know that Queen Victoria chose a gold serpent with emerald eyes for her wedding ring? And that amethyst, a purple variety of quartz, was once believed to bring peace of mind and prevent the wearer from getting drunk?

While the "big three"—emeralds, sapphires, and rubies—remain the most popular, other stones are just as beautiful. Perhaps your favorite color or birthstone is a green emerald, but an emerald is just not in your budget. Take a look at a green tourmaline, which will provide you with a wonderful green stone for much less money.

Another reason antique rings are becoming popular is that many of them were set in white gold. Yellow gold was used to a lesser extent. "I wear more silver than gold and so do my friends," says Rebecca Hanley of Boulder, a twenty-something woman who is getting married in June. "I'm looking for an antique wedding ring in platinum to go with my engagement ring, which is white gold."

Special Care and Repair

When selecting a colored stone as an engagement ring, one that you will wear daily, be concerned about the hardness of the stone. For example, peridot would not be a good choice. It's a soft stone and scratches easily. Even the popular emerald, which is hard, is prone to damage because it is brittle.

In fact, be cautious about the condition of antique and estate pieces before buying. No matter how dazzling a ring, "It's no good if you can't wear it," says Maggie Cronin of Bill Cronin Goldsmith shop in Boulder. "You'll find pieces, which haven't been worn much, and many that have been well loved."

An Edwardian ring of sapphire and diamonds dates to 1901–1910.

Repairs such as reshanking, replacing the back of the worn-out band and retipping, and putting in a new prong, are possible. But it's not possible to rebuild the side structure of a ring, which can wear away when two rings, such as a wedding band and an engagement ring, rub together for a long time. In that case Cronin says, "When the value of the antique piece is no longer there, you may want to remove Grandma's diamond and have it reset. You'll still have Grandma's diamond, but you'll have given it a fresh start."

As for care and cleaning, always go to a reputable jeweler. An ultrasonic cleaner will not hurt diamonds and hard stones, such as sapphires and rubies. It will hurt an emerald. Also, you can clean your antique jewelry at home with jewelry cleaner or a mild liquid soap, a soft cloth, and warm water. Let the piece dry before putting it away. Never rub briskly or use anything abrasive.

In the nineteenth and early twentieth centuries, engagement and wedding rings departed from the plain gold wedding band. Seeking out that special piece, which comes with an unspoken history, is just part of the fun of buying an antique ring or any antique piece of jewelry. Wearing and enjoying it and then passing it on to the next generation is one of life's greatest pleasures.

RESOURCES

DEALERS AND RESTORATION

Bill Cronin Goldsmith, 1235 Alpine Avenue, Boulder, 80304; 303-440-4222; www.billcronin.com.

Classic Facets, 942 Pearl Street, Boulder, 80302; 303-938-8851.

Dave's Gold & Silver Exchange, 548 South Broadway, Denver, 80209; 303-778-6076.

Manhattan West Timeless Jewelry, 1448 South Broadway, Denver, 80210; 303-722-0671.

Somewhere in Time, 1417 South Broadway, Denver, 80210; 303-777-3659.

The Treasured Scarab, 25 East Dakota Avenue, Denver, 80209; 303-777-6884.

Victoriana, 1512 Larimer Street, in Writer Square, Denver, 80202; 303-573-5049.

■ Pottery: A Bouquet of Roseville

by CAROL WARD

There is nothing worse to decide to collect than something that may be beautiful but unavailable—due to scarcity or cost. Tiffany glass lamps by Louis Comfort Tiffany and Tiffany Studios are incredible works of art, but many are already in private collections and museums. When you do find them in shops and at antique shows, be prepared to pay your house downpayment or another hefty sum for the small but lovely light it will shed in your home. Perhaps at one time they were affordable, but now they are out of reach for many of us.

The 1946 Zephyr Lily line came in several shades of Bermuda blue.

Roseville Pottery, too, is going up in price, but it is still affordable. The company was in business a long time and was quite prolific. In the early part of the twentieth century, the Roseville Pottery Company produced work that was aesthetically appealing, well made, well marked, and plentiful.

The company opened in 1891 in Roseville, Ohio, then moved several years later to Zanesville, Ohio, a small town on the Muskingum River.

"A couple of years ago I heard that Roseville was the second most collectible item behind Beanie Babies," says antiques dealer Tanya Cooper of T.L.C. Antiques in Colorado Springs. "The pottery itself has a really nice look. A lot of people's mothers collected it and had it around. It may not have

Most Roseville ceramics were in matte finish with floral designs.

appealed to them as kids, but now that they are older they realize it has beautiful lines, color, the molds are very nice, and florals are popular again."

At local Colorado shows, collectors look for the Columbine line, Tanya says. "Being the state flower, it is highly sought after in this part of the country."

Blessed with huge clay beds and an abundance of natural gas to fire the kilns, the rich clay valley of Ohio nurtured American pottery companies. Roseville produced 132 different product lines, an average of two lines a year for nearly sixty-four years. What makes it exciting is that you can find pieces at flea markets, thrift shops, and antique stores.

Know What to Look For

Roseville made thousands of pieces of pottery from molds, most in a matte glaze (not shiny), including numerous vases, flowerpots, interesting wall pockets, ewers (small pitchers), cookie jars, exquisite jardinieres atop fancy pedestals, and unusual bookends.

Floral motifs were the main decoration. Every common flower is depicted in the Roseville line—gardenia, cherry blossom, peony, clematis—including a few unusual ones. For example, there is a Snowberry line, one of the most obscure flowers in all of nature. Blue, green, and brown were the most popular colors.

Flowers weren't the only source of inspiration. There were solid-color rustic pieces created in the early 1900s and sought out today by arts and crafts fans.

Cherubs adorned the 1915 Donatello line and nudes graced the Panel and Silhouette lines. Later, pieces were made in the art deco and moderne styles.

Collectors love the naturalistic Pine Cone line with its pinecones, branches, and needles sweeping down on vases, baskets, and bowls. The Pine Cone line was a big seller when it came out in 1935. Hugely popular, the company brought back the line in 1953.

Some collectors want a piece from each line, others collect one line and search for every piece made in that line. Jan Thomas of Longmont can boast about the three hundred pieces in her collection. She started buying ten years ago. "When I started, I didn't even know I was collecting," Jan says. Then she wanted an example from every pattern. "At this point I only look for special patterns and unusual pieces like the Rozanne paperweights, which I recently acquired." And she watches her budget, too.

Turn the Piece Over

Roseville had an excellent marking system. Although not every piece was marked, most were. Fewer had a Roseville stamp pasted on, which in time fell off. By simply turning over the piece, you will learn a lot. Specifically, the name Roseville and U.S.A. are written on the bottom, along with a number—usually three digits—cataloging the shape, and a number indicating the piece's size in inches.

The columbine flower is a favorite among Colorado collectors.

This information is immensely helpful because it allows you to look up the piece in a Roseville book. There are several excellent ones on the market. Match the line, number, and size, and you can figure out exactly what piece you have, what it is called, the year it was made, and the present market value. The company kept a record of its wares, factory stock, and even the artists' names.

Another helpful hint when identifying Roseville is in the color of the clay. On the unpainted bottom you will notice that Roseville Pottery was made with a particular clay that, when fired, turned a beige to a light golden brown color.

Variations in Color and Molds

Although there is continuity throughout Roseville Pottery, each piece was not created equal, even within the same line. For example, let's take two large vases of the Zephyr Lily line in the color of Bermuda blue. "A lovely floral design of unusual grace, beauty and refinement" read an advertisement in the publication *Gift and Buyer* in January 1946. One vase may be lighter in color, the other a somewhat darker blue. Is one better than the other? No. In this case, it's personal preference that matters.

Less common were small vases with figures that Roseville produced for art deco designs in 1910.

However, one vase may be sharper in detail than the other. The lilies and leaves may be crisper and stand out more sharply on one vase. On the other vase, the flowers may be dull and not as well defined. This variation is due to the mold. The dull piece may have been set in an older mold, and the crisp piece was probably set in a new and fresher mold. In this case, there is indeed a difference in the quality of the two pieces, and it should be reflected in the price tag.

Always look for a sharp crisp piece with a motif as distinctive and detailed as possible. At least be sure that your piece is commensurate with the asking price because beauty, after all, is in the eye of the beholder.

The Pine Cone line, which came out in 1935, was an instant hit.

Places to Buy

I've already mentioned antique and thrift shops. Attend auctions, where prices should be lower than in antique shops. Get the hammer prices from auctions. You can usually get a computer printout for a small fee after each auction.

The Internet makes buying somewhat more accessible, Tanya says. "You can find on the other side of the country what you may not see or find locally through a single show." A free and up-to-the-minute price guide is constantly available on the Internet: register at www.ebay.com and then conduct a search for Roseville.

Survey your own home and your friends' homes. Don't be surprised when you turn over a flowerpot that you've been looking at for years and find that it is Roseville. Mothers, grandmothers, and aunts have been buying Roseville for generations. The price was certainly right in the early days. Ads from the 1900s show pieces selling for $3.00 to $5.00, $11.50, and $18.00, to cite a normal price range. Today, those same pieces, if you can find them, are worth so much more.

An advertisement in 1905 for a size 16¼-inch "Egypto" vase no. E68 with birds cost $18. Today the value of that piece is between $1,800 and $2,200. But this is rare and on the higher end of the Roseville scale. Today, you can find wonderful moderate mint condition pieces of Roseville (first-quality ware with a normal amount of crazing and no serious defects) in shops ranging on average from $150 to $600. Also look for Roseville at estate sales.

"I've just seen prices increasing," says Tanya. "There's no reason to expect them to decrease." What worries Tanya and others are reproductions. "What I hate to see is Roseville being heavily reproduced. That could affect prices a bit."

Reproductions and Restoration

According to Tanya, the reproductions that she has seen have been very poor. "Anyone who has collected it or seen much of Roseville can recognize the reproductions very quickly. The molding is pretty good but the paint is terrible. It doesn't have the delicate, muted, very pretty colors that Roseville has. The colors are much more harsh, the painting isn't good. If you set a reproduction next to a real piece you can tell immediately. I haven't seen any really good reproductions that would fool someone. But I don't like the fact that it's being done."

As for restoration, Mark Nilsson has been working on china, porcelain, and pottery for three years, under his moniker China Man: "If the work is done properly it should last the life of the piece. Remember that restoration involves the use of epoxy, painting, and reglazing, but the piece will not be refired. So, as long as you use the piece decoratively only, it should be fine." The cost of restoration depends on the damaged piece but is affordable. For example, Nilsson says a chip of one color would cost about $25 to fix. Restoring ewer spouts starts at $65.

After a piece is restored, the owner or dealer is generally able to get 75 to 80 percent of its original value if the restoration is done well. "The restoration should be invisible," says Nilsson. A reputable dealer will let a customer know that a piece has been restored. The price should reflect the restoration and therefore be that much lower.

At shops and shows, ask the dealer if you may pick up a piece. Touch it, turn it over, feel the finish. Beyond the piece's physicality, discovering who, where, and when make the pieces you are acquiring much more interesting.

Begin by researching Roseville, and you'll uncover an important era of America's craft heritage.

RESOURCES

Crooksville–Roseville Pottery Festival, Annual Collectible Pottery Sale, Ohio Ceramic Center, 7327 Ceramic Road, Roseville, Ohio 43777; 800-752-2604; www.potteryfestival.org/. For true Roseville Pottery fans; usually held in July.

Laguna Vintage Pottery, 116 South Washington Street, Seattle, Washington 98104; 206-682-6162; www.lagunapottery.com.

In addition, you'll find Roseville sprinkled throughout antique stores in Colorado, especially those devoted to glass and pottery.

RECOMMENDED READING

Understanding Roseville Pottery by Mark Bassett; order at www.markbassett.com. Comes with a price guide.

ARTUS VAN BRIGGLE: MASTER OF ARTS AND CRAFTS POTTERY

by DIANNE ZUCKERMAN

Earth, water, and fire are pottery's essential elements. How appropriate, then, for the art form to flourish in a city so in harmony with these elements, from distinctive red-toned bluffs to freshwater mountain lakes to the searing high-country sun.

Colorado Springs beckoned to Artus Van Briggle in 1899. The Ohio-born artist came in hopes that the salubrious mountain climate would restore his health. Unfortunately, the quest proved elusive for the talented painter and potter, who died of tuberculosis in 1904, at age thirty-five. Although Van Briggle's life was cut tragically short, he left behind a rich artistic legacy. Today, the still-active Van Briggle Pottery produces a wealth of vases, lamps, decorative tiles, and other items.

Artus Van Briggle's floral tiles are typical of the art nouveau style.

Many of these are reproductions of Van Briggle's lauded original works. Today, original pieces are sought by private collectors and also can be found at museums such as the Smithsonian Institution, the Metropolitan Museum of Art, and the British Museum. The largest Van Briggle collection on public display can be seen at the Colorado Springs Pioneers Museum.

Original Van Briggle pieces, which sell for thousands of dollars, may be out of reach for the average aficionado. But those drawn to Van Briggle's distinctive style—rich colors, flowing lines and designs that lean toward classical figures, and a profusion of floral patterns—can acquire reproductions made at a studio that also welcomes visitors who want to learn more about the pottery-making process.

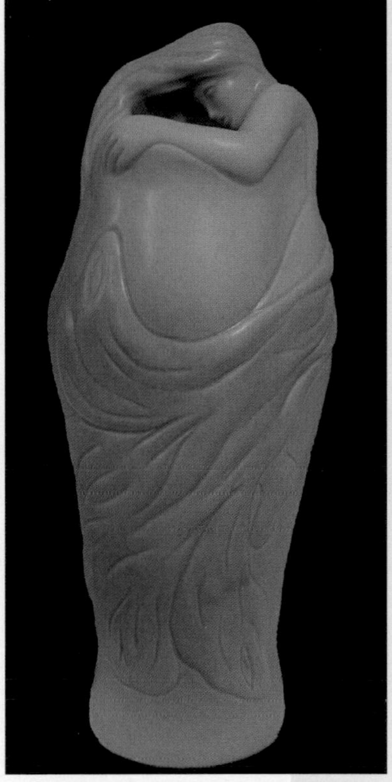

The "Lorelei" vase may be Artus Van Briggle's most recognized work.

Studio Continues Van Briggle Work

A historic, semicircular stone building that once served as the roundhouse for the Midland Railroad now houses the sprawling Van Briggle Pottery studio, which offers free self-guided tours. The facility, which turns out some thirty thousand pieces a year and ships its wares around the world, is one of only a few studios in the United States that still hand-pours such a large number of works.

It all began with Artus Van Briggle, whose creations were recognized at various international exhibitions during his time. He also gained fame for his painstaking rediscovery of an ancient Chinese matte glaze, which added luster to designs that were influenced by the art nouveau style.

Art nouveau, which was popular toward the end of the nineteenth century and into the first decade of the twentieth, was part of the arts and crafts movement and emphasized undulating forms, such as curving plant tendrils and a woman's free-flowing hair.

Van Briggle's most popular design, the "Lorelei" vase, embodies this style. Based on the German myth about a lovelorn maiden who threw herself into the Rhine River, the "Lorelei" incorporates a female figure whose arms and flowing locks form the top of the vase. "Despondency," his other best-known design, also reflects this style, as a despairing male figure is sculpted along the top of a vase in a way that makes the form seem to emerge organically from the piece.

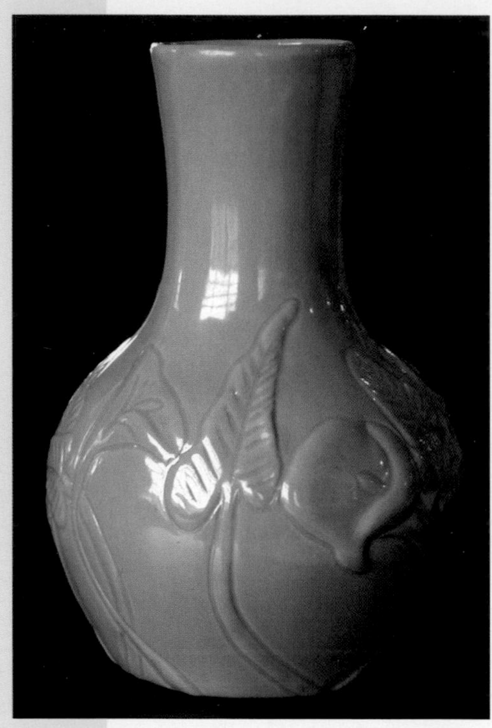
The majority of studio pieces are hand-poured slip casting.

Van Briggle first learned his craft at the Rookwood Pottery Company in Ohio. Recognizing his talent and promise, the owners of the Cincinnati studio sent him abroad for additional studies. While on a trip to Paris, he met Anne Gregory, a painter who later followed him to Colorado in 1900. After marrying in 1902, they worked together to establish Van Briggle Pottery. Their joint effort is reflected in the company's trademark logo, a pair of linked *A*'s locked together inside a square.

An exhibit at the studio traces the couple's work and relationship. The display also includes numerous original Van Briggle pieces and historic photographs of early artisans at work, their solemn expressions and highly proper hats and caps giving them a stiff, formal look.

The exhibit is surrounded by several large work areas where today's artisans carry on the tradition of crafting decorative pottery. Videotapes located in each section explain the various steps.

Studio Tour Explains the Process

Van Briggle Pottery still turns out a limited number of hand-thrown original pots. But the majority of pieces are made by hand-poured slip casting, a method used to produce a pottery design in quantity. Slip is made from a basic clay mixed with other minerals and water in huge mechanized vats called blungers.

"What makes our clay work at our temperatures and [with] our glazes is the chemicals that we add to it," explains Mark Sucharski, an artisan whose work includes firing the kilns used to strengthen and glaze the pieces.

The slip is poured into plaster molds. At present, Van Briggle uses over two hundred molds, which are lined up on long tables that fill the slip-casting section. The highly absorbent molds draw out excess moisture, which causes the slip to thicken. This in turn creates layers that conform to each individual mold. "Ideally, if your slip is just right, it's about an hour," Mark notes about the formation process.

After the slip casting is complete and the pieces have been removed from the molds, which come apart in sections, the next step is the etching room. Large windows provide a good view of the process. Several women sit at long tables, using etching tools to trim off seams formed in the molds. They also enhance various design details, such as a columbine—Colorado's state flower—that graces a vase.

After the etchers complete their work, the pieces, considered to be in a greenware state, are placed onto a cart and loaded into the bisque kiln for the first firing. The process lasts about four hours and reaches a temperature of 1,700 degrees. The purpose of this firing is to strengthen the pots and prepare them for glazing.

Artus Van Briggle's studio continues with the same techniques the artist practiced more than 100 years ago.

Gary Dhondt, who oversees the glazing process, has been with the company since 1995. He learned his craft directly from Craig Stevenson, Van Briggle's vice president and master sculptor. Following Van Briggle's traditional style, Stevenson has created such works as a series of American Indian busts and the company's commemorative centennial piece, the "Four Seasons" vase.

"He personally taught me the technique of dipping, because every piece you handle a little bit differently when you submerge it in glaze," Gary says. "The object is to get as few runs as possible, because the sprayers have to take those runs or drips off."

Tiles have become a major portion of the studio's output today.

Like other steps in the pottery-making process, glazing is labor-intensive. After the initial dipping, "they put the piece on a turntable and rotate it by hand," Gary explains. "And after they take off any little bumps or runs, they'll spray on additional glaze." The pieces are then placed in another kiln for the second firing. This takes about eight hours at 2,200 degrees and brings out the various colors, which range from soft lilac to warm turquoise. Some of the older glazes are no longer produced because of the high lead content in the clay. Today, all Van Briggle Pottery meets government lead-free standards.

Each tile is a stylized flower—tulips and lilies are favorites.

Decorative Tiles Remain Popular

The studio also produces numerous decorative tiles embellished with floral images. The pieces recall a period during the 1930s and 1940s when tile production was a major part of the studio's output. It was a time when upscale local homes often boasted decorative tiles as accents on fireplaces, floors, and walls.

The walk-through tour ends in a spacious showroom filled with a wide range of items, from a simple bud vase for under $20 to more elaborate and expensive vases, lamps, and pitchers. But don't look for a bargain table bearing imperfect items. Every piece sold at Van Briggle must meet quality control standards. Those that don't pass muster never make it out of the workroom.

"I break the ones we can't use," notes Mark, the artisan whose responsibilities include examining finished pieces. "You can't buy seconds."

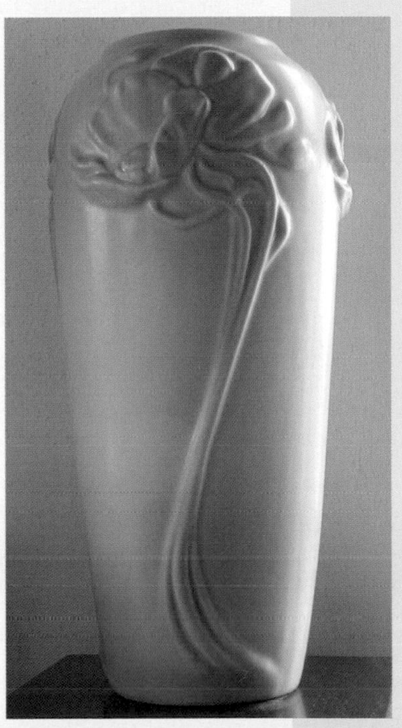

Artus Van Briggle discovered an ancient Chinese matte glaze that is associated with his work.

RESOURCES

The Colorado Arts & Crafts Society, c/o The Boettcher Mansion, Lookout Mountain Nature Preserve, 900 Coloraw Road, Golden, 80401; 303-526-0855. A world-class example of arts and crafts architecture and home of the society.

The Colorado Springs Pioneers Museum, 217 South Tejon Street, Colorado Springs, 80903; 719-385-5990; www.springsgov.com (click on the Cultural Services section).

The Crafted Home; 303-860-8444; www.thecraftedhome.com. Home furnishings and accessories devoted to the arts and crafts movement.

Van Briggle Pottery, 600 South 21st Street, Colorado Springs, 80904; 800-847-6341; www.vanbriggle.com. Open 8:30 A.M. to 5 P.M., Monday through Saturday, and seasonally on Sundays.

RECOMMENDED READING

The Collector's Encyclopedia of Van Briggle Art Pottery by Richard Sasicki and Josie Fania (Collector Books, 1992). Provides information about the history of the company and its wealth of designs.

ANTIQUE LINENS: THE EXTRAVAGANCE OF NEEDLE ART

by CAROL WARD

My eye first settled on the antique iron bed made only more beautiful by the crisp, snowy white linens draped elegantly over the sides. Although 90 percent of Paula Gins' linens are English, she buys from other places in Europe and sells at shows in Colorado and around the country.

It was a quick but big step when Paula went from selling shoes to buying and selling antique linens. A former shoe company executive, Paula left the garment district in New York, moved to Denver with her husband, and entered the Victorian era. Now she buys linens worldwide and keeps a huge inventory of antique bedspreads, pillowcases, shams, tablecloths, hand towels, and doilies, which were all handmade between 1820 and 1890. At the zenith of the British Industrial Revolution, looms produced exceptional textiles—densely woven with crisp surfaces that served as canvases for needlework.

Embroidery reached a zenith in the nineteenth century for European linens.

The nineteenth century "was the most prolific in producing this type of handwork," Paula says. "Great skill was executed by the women who produced these pieces. Everything was hand done—crocheted and embroidered. The materials were the best cottons and linens of the time."

Paula knew that she was onto something when she sold a few insignificant but lovely linens at a local antiques show in 1984. When

Paula realized she was out of merchandise, in a moment of serendipity, a woman walked up to her booth and gave her names to use as contacts to buy more.

Most of Paula's linens come from old manor estates and fine country homes in England. Her contacts call her when the heirs, who often can't keep up the fine old manor homes, are ready to sell the contents. She travels to Europe three or four times a year. That's how she manages to find quantity as well as quality.

Elaborate linens have been folded and stored for years in Europe's manor estates.

Once a year, Paula opens her suburban home, and the lower level becomes a display room. Antique dressers and tables are stacked high with dozens of cotton and linen tablecloths and bedspreads—all white.

The large room is set up with a decorator's eye. Adorning the top of the bed are lace-edged embroidered pillows. One in particular has a blue hand-embroidered bird. Though a small pillow has been made to place inside, Gins explained that originally it was a nightdress case: "Girls in the convent were taught to sew, and one of their first projects was to make a container to hold their nightgown. In fact, it was their sampler."

Linens Stamped by Towns of Origin

Quite a few embroidery styles were named for the area where they originated. There are beautifully embroidered pillowcases from Italy, and Appenzell linens from Switzerland. Appenzell is fine embroidery recognizable by the distinctive punchwork grid that gives it a "lace" appearance.

Appenzell linens are usually detailed figurative pieces, such as a woman with pearls around her neck or the face of a woman with flowing hair. "These

Appenzell linens look much like cameos complete with figures and painstaking detail.

types of cameos are very rare," Gins says. One Appenzell tablecloth in particular, with buttonhole and seed stitch, is valued at $950.

Fewer in number but a part of her collection are the Madeira pieces from Portugal. The island of Madeira is renowned for its embroideries and lace work—punched-out eyelets finished on the edges with a satin stitch. It's a hand technique widely adapted to contemporary commercial flounces on bedspreads and ruffles.

Cream-colored curtains from France are folded neatly on the end of one table. Several long christening dresses hang from the window. These antique baby gowns from the 1800s are in practically pristine condition, with no one dress exactly alike.

A Vocabulary of Skills

Embroidery and lace terms fill the room—*French knot, punchwork, cutwork, filet, tatting, bobbin lace,* and *spider weaving.* There is also drawnwork, where the seamstress actually removes threads from the fabric. A "forbidden" stitch appears on Chinese embroidery. "The thread had to be kept wet and the lighting dark while the sewing was done," Paula says. The conditions were so extreme that needleworkers, usually young girls, went blind in its execution and so it became forbidden work by Chinese imperial command.

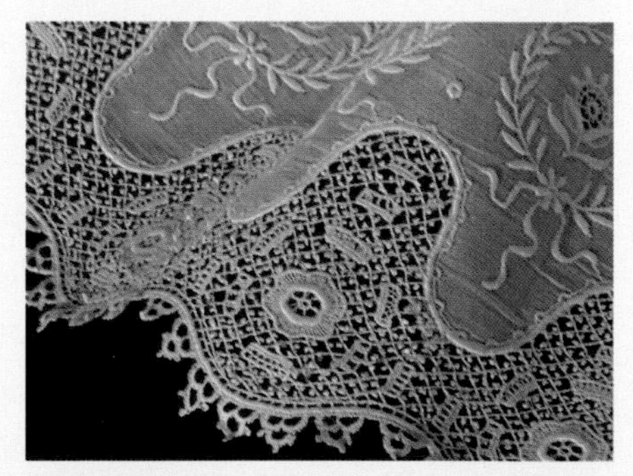

The trimmed edge of a christening gown indicates how important the event was for a family.

Some pieces tell a story, such as the harp and shamrock handkerchief found in a trousseau. The bride's wedding veil and handkerchief are lace; the names of the couple married in Ireland in 1846 are embroidered on the hanky.

Paula points to a piece of Irish linen called Mountmellick. This embroidered linen appeared about 1830 as a way for local Irish women to earn enough money to live during times of declining prosperity.

The Irish shamrock shows up throughout Irish linens as a trademark of their embroidery.

It was the wealthy who could afford these finer things, so it frequently fell to the poor women—young and often orphaned girls in convents, women who became pregnant out of wedlock in England, Ireland, and other countries—to sew for the upper classes. In general, though, women sewed, learning and passing on techniques from mother to daughter.

A Labor of Love

As for the prices on her wares—"They are not inexpensive," Paula acknowledges. "If someone wants them, they'll pay for them because they know that they'll never find something like this again. There's a crisp feel to the old fabrics. These are all pure fabrics and the handwork cannot be duplicated today."

Paula's customers often are young women who were given a piece of lace by their mothers or grandmothers and want to expand on that. Or, they are women in their fifties whose linens are wearing out and they want to replace them.

If you are lucky and find antique linens, look for pieces with no repairs or weak spots by holding them up to the light. Paula agrees that it's a lot of work to restore the luster of linens, but you'll be surprised at how well old linens hold up with the right kind of care.

Caring for Antique Linens

WASHING

Use your washing machine on gentle cycle with cold water. For a small load, add ½ scoop of powder detergent, ⅛ cup of La France whitener (a bluing), and 1 scoop of OxiClean (a nonchlorinated bleach). Agitate the machine until the laundry products are dissolved, and then add the linens. In the last deep-water rinse add ½ cup of white vinegar, which will remove any residue that may be left in the fabric.

Young girls embroidered samplers that later were made into pillows.

DRYING AND IRONING

Use your dryer on the gentle or permanent press cycle, or line dry. Do not dampen. Set your dry iron (remove any water from iron) on the middle setting. Pad your ironing board with several white cotton Turkish towels.

REMOVING STAINS

Soak in a small amount of powder detergent and Biz for several hours in a glass bowl. For extra whitening, dissolve detergent and Biz in a porcelain pot and simmer for ten to twenty minutes, then follow washing instructions. Wash all your matching napkins to keep them the same color. To remove wine, candle wax, or coffee stains, pour hot water through the fabric from the wrong side.

STORING

For linens that will not be used regularly, put them washed without pressing in a cotton pillowcase. If the case is new, wash to remove the sizing. This will keep them free of dust until you are ready to iron them.

RESOURCES

DEALERS

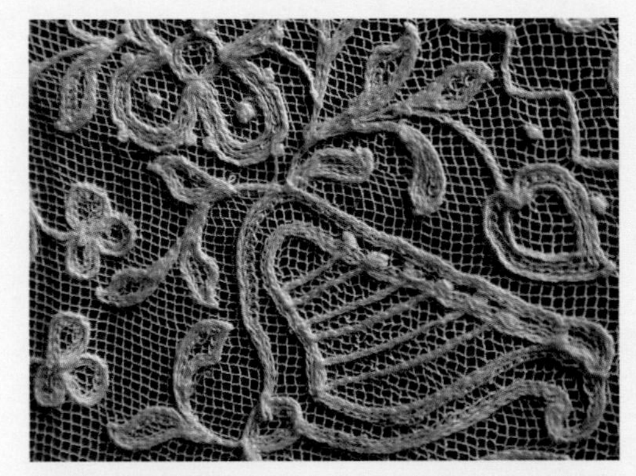

A distinctively Irish harp and shamrock handkerchief was part of a bride's trousseau.

The Apiary (Jean Snow), 585 Milwaukee Street, Denver, 80206; 303-399-6017. Jean carries a selection of tablecloths, sheets, napkins, runners, French linens like toile (printed fabric with scenes of French rustic life in 1700s), pillows; most linens date from the 1800s and to present day.

The Collection (Bette Rossen), 899 Broadway, Denver, 80203; 303-623-4200; www.antiquedesign.com. Nineteenth and twentieth century up to the 1950s; European bedding to quilts, coverlets, paisley shawls, lace, baby gifts, christening gowns, vintage fabric, trim.

Paula Gins Antique Linens; 303-734-9095; e-mail: paulaginsantiquelinens@msn.com. Paula also sells at the Denver Mart's World Wide Antiques Show; www.wwantiqueshows.com.

Warner's Antiques (Mariella Warner), 1401 South Broadway, Denver, 80210; 303-722-9173; www.warnersantiques.com. Wide selection, carries nineteenth- and twentieth-century linens, up to 1920.

RECOMMENDED READING

Caring for Textiles by Karen Finch and Greta Putnam (Watson-Guptill, 1977).

■ Silver: A Grandmother's Legacy

by CAROL WARD

The unusual silver serving utensil felt soft and cool in my hand. The detail in the pattern was interesting and well executed, but I hadn't a clue as to what it was. That is, what was it used for? The piece belonged to a set of silver flatware. With a wonderful acorn design at the top, the long handle came to a very round, very flat end. It looked like something that you would use to flip a small pancake. And so it sat—beautiful, elegant, and sterling—much too nice to be put away in a drawer.

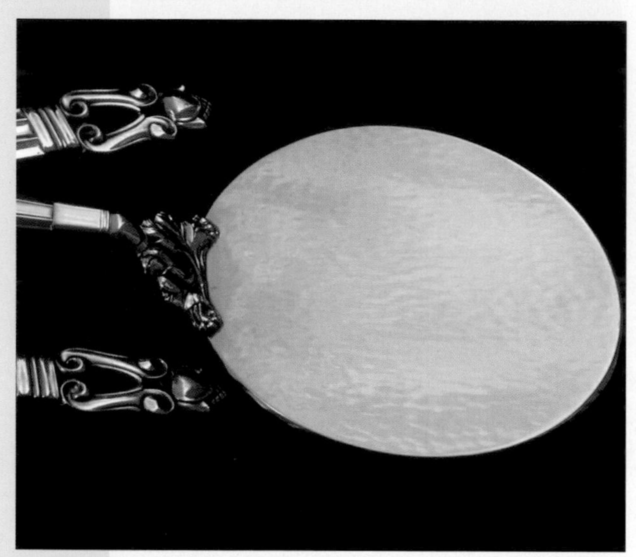

The Victorians delighted in silver pieces for the most specialized purposes. This is a tomato slice server.

To find out about my mystery spatula, I headed to the local bookstore for a good book on silver. Knowing a few antiques dealers in the neighborhood, I stopped by to chat with them. I learned a great deal that day about my flatware, a Victorian tomato server, and a great deal more about silverware.

Silver flatware and silver serving pieces come in numerous patterns made by a multitude of silver makers and silver manufacturing companies. And while there is an abundance of silver flatware, the more unique serving utensils and flatware are becoming difficult to find. Many of these unusual, rare pieces were made in the mid- to late 1800s, during the Victorian era.

Silver Remains Valuable

Handsome ladles were common for soups or gravies and are among the most interesting shapes.

"There were so many exciting periods for silver, and every one of them is absolutely fascinating," says Marie Brown, a Boulder antiques dealer. "The study of silver can take the rest of your life." People simply like silver—for its beauty, history, and inherent value. "Silver is never going to be worthless," Marie says, "because it's a precious metal." Marie has specialized in silver for more than thirty years. Currently, silver is fascinating for another reason: it's selling low at $4.40 an ounce. Silver, like many other precious metals, fluctuates. "It will go up eventually," she predicts.

Sterling silver is made with 925 parts silver out of 1,000 parts of metal, often copper or nickel. When you see *sterling* or *925* stamped on an item, it meets the silver industry's high silver content standard. Silver once was a highly regulated commodity, so the mark is a quality guarantee adopted by the United States after about 1860, although England and Ireland noted sterling earlier. It is more valuable than silver plate or electroplate because a higher content of silver is used in the piece, which will wear better and last much longer. Oh, yes, it will cost a little more, too.

The fish decorations on these spatula handles indicate that they are fish servers.

Finding Serving and Flatware Pieces

Mothers, mothers-in-law, and grandmothers, passing their sets down to the next generation, are excellent sources of silver flatware. Antique shops, auctions, and estate sales are all good places to locate and buy silver. A "good eye" may reward you at a flea market. Don't pass by a store or a booth at an antiques show just because they don't specialize in silver flatware. These are the shops and people who may have just one or two pieces, don't really care about them, and may not know the exact market value. It's challenging to find these odd utensils and more so to get them at a good price (translation: it won't break the bank). But the work involved will be worth it because they are absolutely gorgeous. Many of the early pieces were handwork—tooled by hand and not just stamped out. As in the case of Gorham Silver Company, men who worked first as silversmiths learning their craft founded a number of manufacturing companies. Jabez Gorham started his apprenticeship in 1807. Then in 1815, he began producing under his own name and developed his own company, which is still in production today.

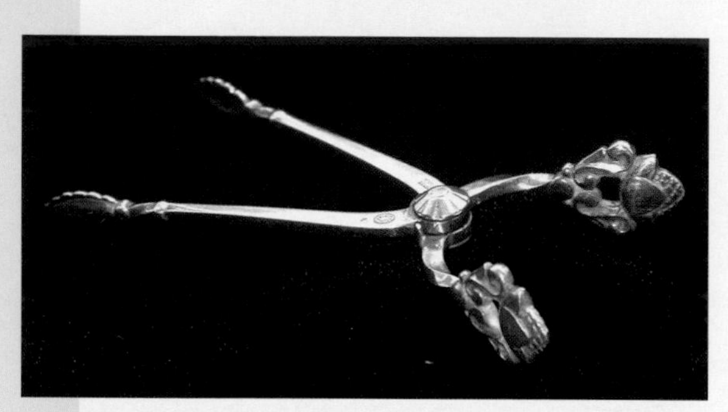

Elaborate tongs were used for pickles, olives, nuts, and ice.

These pieces will be stunning on your dinner table, but there aren't very many left. Sadly, much silver was melted down during the 1980s when silver was at a premium.

Manufacturers are no longer making these unusual pieces because people simply stopped using them. So, if you find them, you will have pieces that your friends don't have—and never will.

Victorian silver often is beautifully detailed.

Victorian Abundance

The Victorians had a utensil for just about every kind of food. Marie cites a Victorian set that consisted of twenty-four-piece place settings. That's twenty-four pieces of flatware for just one person!

Did you think that a simple spoon was always used for ice cream? There are indeed ice-cream forks, too. Ice-cream forks are half spoon, half fork. Ice cream was very hard back then, stored on blocks of ice. "Ice-cream spoons are hard to find because they are not part of a modern set and companies don't make them today," Marie says. Ice-cream knives went along with them to cut the ice cream. Then there are cheese scoop servers that look like shovels and individual cheese scoops that look like tiny shovels to scoop cheese. To eat your turtle soup you'd use a special utensil called a terrapin fork.

It's surprising how many different kinds of asparagus serving pieces were required, from pierced flat surfaces to forks to tongs. I'm happy to know that others, in earlier times, were as confused as I am about how to serve asparagus.

Baby spoons have bent handles.

Toast servers, sandwich tongs, cracker scoops, and nut spoons all kept hands clean.

Ladles are some of the prettiest pieces, very sculptural in design. So many ladles for gravy, sauce, cream, oysters,

These small berry spoons reveal berries etched into the silver.

soup, and punch. Olive, pickle, fish, and salad forks. Berry, sugar, soup, and jelly spoons. Butter spreaders, butter picks, and butter knives. Carving sets, poultry shears, and servers of all kinds—it's a long and amazing list.

Change over the years makes many utensils unnecessary, even obsolete. With some unusual utensils a decorative pattern reveals a clue as to their use: a fish design on the handle of a fish server, berries etched into a berry spoon. Others may remain mysterious unless you understand how foods have changed. Today, we use a saltshaker instead of a saltcellar and salt spoon.

The refining of chocolate no longer necessitates a chocolate spoon or muddler to stir the once concentrated chocolate liquid. We use our hands to pick up nuts, sandwiches, and toast. And if one utensil can do several jobs, so be it. Life should be less complicated, but why hide such artistic pieces? Give them a second life.

Dinner parties are a great opportunity to show off. Dust off the fine china and crystal glasses and put beautiful sterling silver on your table. Serve the salad with a lovely set of salad servers. Use your tomato server to pick up baked potatoes, cucumbers, and even tomatoes. Get Grandmother's set of strawberry forks to eat the strawberries on your strawberry shortcake and place a beautiful dessert fork next to it. Stir espresso with demitasse spoons. How lovely the table will look as your sterling silver reflects the candlelight.

Silver Marks and Patterns

Of all antiques and collectibles, silver is the best marked. When you turn over a piece of silverware, you're likely to see the silver content and the manufacturer. On English silver you're also likely to see the place of origin and a date mark. A good book on silver hallmarks can help you trace just about any piece of hallmarked silver.

Patterns and silver companies abound, making it hard to choose a pattern. Two very old patterns, Buttercup and Chantilly, both by Gorham, are two of the most popular patterns. People love them, and they are still being made today.

Collectors collect what they love. Some want every type of asparagus server and don't even need to use them. Many collectors like little pieces such as sugar tongs, small ice tongs, sterling silver baby spoons, and tiny salt spoons for their saltcellars—a trend revisited. Others buy pieces to add to their sets and to replace lost or damaged pieces.

Silver is making a comeback, mixing with informal dinnerware.

For silver flatware replacements, people often look to a North Carolina company called Replacements. You can look them up (see the Resources section at the end of this chapter), and you'll also see their ads in many national magazines.

Prices in Today's Market—Price Guides

Price guides are "guides" for pricing and not the final word on items. Prices vary according to rarity and the condition of the piece, market fluctuations, and geographical regions. Even a television segment can influence prices on items. And guide lists on sterling pieces indicate what you might expect to pay in the current marketplace: a tomato server by Gorham in the pattern of Villa Norfolk is valued at $125.

Old silver combines beauty, history, and value. It's wonderful to own it and nice to share it with others at your dinner table. And as Marie Brown says, "Food just tastes better in silver."

RESOURCES

■ DEALERS

Bennett Antiques, 1220 South College, Fort Collins, 80524; 970-482-3645; www.bennettantiques.com.

Bedell & Co., 767 Pearl Street, Boulder, 80302; 303-939-9292; www.bedellandco.com. Silver is a specialty.

Black Tulip Antiques, Ltd., 1370 South Broadway, Denver, 80210; 303-777-1370.

McDowell's Antiques, 1400 South Broadway, Denver, 80210; 303-777-0601; www.mcdowellantiques.com. Silver is a specialty.

Powder Cache Antiques, 612 Sixth Street, Unit C, Georgetown, 80444; 303-569-2848; http://antiques-internet.com/colorado/powdercacheantiques/PP02.htm. Artifacts connected to mining days; also a private museum devoted to the silver mining history of Georgetown and Silver Plume.

■ RECOMMENDED READING

Kovels' Antiques & Collectibles Price List by Ralph Kovel and Terry Kovel (Three Rivers Press, published annually). Also, online pricing guide at www.kovels.com.

Yesterday's Silver for Today's Table: A Silver Collector's Guide to Elegant Dining by Richard Osterberg (Schiffer Publishing, 2001).

■ JUDGED BY THEIR COVERS: THE WORLD OF ANCIENT AND RARE BOOKS

by NIKI HAYDEN

Hold a book of poetry by Katibi of Nishapur in your hands and you might guess where it originated. The design of the page resembles the intricacies of a Middle Eastern carpet. A fluid, stylized script floats delicately on paper in ink, gold leaf, and blue lapis lazuli. The date is 1605. The place is Persia.

Contrast that small, personal book to one by William Morris. It's a large, hand-set, printed book with a heavy black font resembling Gothic lettering. Dated 1896 by Kelmscott Press, only 425 copies were printed. Fewer have survived.

These beauties are among the thousands in the Special Collections room at the University of Colorado's Norlin Library in Boulder. It's a museum for books—from the collection of late-eighteenth-century British women poets to the prints of twentieth-century American landscape photographer Ansel Adams.

Care to see a four-thousand-year-old cuneiform clay tablet? It's a merchant's receipt from the Sumerian city of Ur. Or perhaps you'd prefer to see something more recent, like an artist's book disguised as a box of candy. And then there are miniatures, like a tiny Hebrew book from Poland that comes with a magnifying glass on the cover.

A book of poetry by Katibi of Nishapur dates to 1605.

From the ancient to the contemporary, the collection cuts a wide swath in book history and reveals cultures long buried. You'll find the valuable, such as a 1450s' leaf from a Gutenberg Bible. And you'll find the despicable: Adolf Hitler signed and dated a copy of his book *Mein Kampf* in 1935. A nineteenth-century child's reading primer is steeped in racist language. Such documents, librarian Deborah Hollis says, are cultural artifacts. They're not prized for intrinsic worth, which may be very little, but because they reveal the thinking of the day. Lose these, and you'll lose a historical truth.

A Book Is Judged by Its Condition and Cultural Context

Usually, when it comes to collecting books, condition is paramount. Students wear white gloves as they turn the pages. Books rest in wooden cradles. "The more pristine the book, the more valuable it will be," Hollis confirms. "This is often difficult to find, especially with children's books. They are so well loved. But our books are cultural artifacts and the value doesn't depend on a rip in a dust jacket. Our books are the product of time and place."

A book by William Morris captures the spirit of the English arts and crafts movement in 1896.

That holds true for many book collectors, too. Carol P. Grossman is a dealer and collector of fine press books—limited editions of books on exquisite paper with etchings by artists, often accompanied by poetry. It's important that her books be in impeccable condition. But that wouldn't be the case for other categories, she says: "A diary written during the Civil War is important no matter the condition."

On the opposite end of the collecting spectrum, the tiniest nick on the dust jacket of a first edition by a popular mystery writer could drop the value by 20 percent. Many dealers handle only first edition popular books, Grossman says, but they don't interest her. She collects books that have been bound in snakeskin with appliqué or silk covers. Perhaps only a hundred were printed. One favorite she opens is *The First Book of Moses Called Genesis,* with silk-screened stencils of paintings by noted artist Jacob Lawrence.

A tiny Hebrew book from Poland includes a magnifying glass.

There is room in the book world for many kinds of collectors, Carol says. No matter how narrow or arcane the focus, there's a group to be found. Once book collecting was in the hands of a tiny circle of devotees, but it's less exclusive these days. In the past, older men with considerable savings made up the clientele. That's because it takes wealth to buy rare books in mass. It still takes money, but the collectors have changed. They're more likely to be younger, between the ages of thirty and forty, embarking on a grand ambition. Women are more prevalent than ever. And collectors now buy slowly and carefully over a long period of time, rather than trying to amass a grand library quickly.

"More women are dealing with the kinds of books I deal in. Perhaps it's because they have to do with the arts," Carol says. "In the past, women didn't have the kind of money it takes to collect books. And it does take an education. But there are all kinds of collectors now. Estelle Doheny, who died about twenty years ago, had an enormous and beautiful collection. But she was wealthy. I find now that serious collectors start early and it becomes a lifelong habit."

All collectors are constricted by budgets and by what's available. Some books simply have disappeared from the public domain. Libraries have built first-class collections in recent years. Once a book is purchased for a library, it will not return to the rare book market. And some specialties, like English poets, have been mined for a long time. Just try to find a first edition of John Milton's *Paradise Lost.*

Carol divides her clients into those who master a tiny slice of publishing—selecting a time period or limited genre of literature—and accumulators who reach out across a broad selection of books. "The accumulators have an omnivorous appetite for reading, but they may not follow a discipline for their collecting," she says.

Getting Started

To get started in book collecting, Carol offers suggestions:

Find something you love. Right now, the hot trend is children's books. They're hard to find in mint condition, but it's a trend with a steady following. That's true for cookbooks, too. Most are well used. Those in pristine condition bring a high price. A first edition of Irma S. Rombauer and Marion Rombauer Becker's *The Joy of Cooking* in excellent shape will bring between $3,000 and $4,000. If you're uncertain about dipping a toe into the sea of books, a good place to start is where you live: consider Colorado literature, diaries, or artifacts.

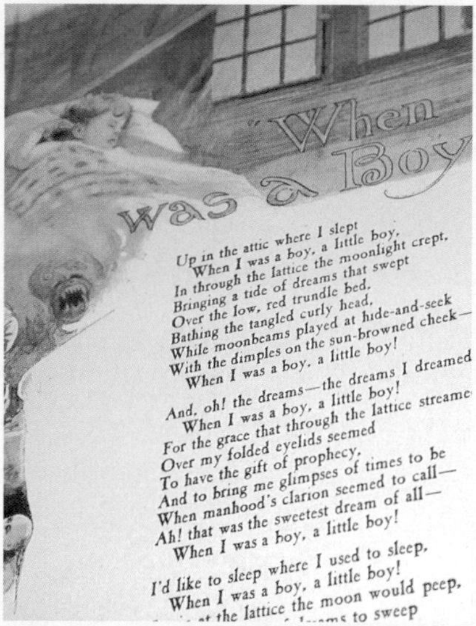

Children's books are a popular collector's item now.

Read everything you can find on the subject you love. Begin in libraries, especially rare book collections, and on the Internet. Don't look with an eye to buy, just to learn. Pick up the vocabulary as well as the history of your chosen field. Always look into bibliographies of books on your subject; they will lead you to more in-depth research.

Find someone knowledgeable who shares your interest. This may be another collector or a librarian. There's someone out there who will love to share a lifetime of experience with you.

Attend book fairs and talk to dealers. Many of them know the field and are happy to talk to you—even if you're not ready to buy just yet.

Okay, you've learned volumes on what you want to collect. Before you plunk down the money, here are a few warnings. Be careful of online auctions. You can't touch what you are buying. The condition may not be as it appears.

Only 425 copies of William Morris's book were published, which makes it all the more valuable.

Also, check the truthfulness of your sources. Is the person you're talking to associated with a credible institution?

Finally, know the terminology. You'll be able to spot some deceptive ads just by the misuse of words and descriptions.

Eventually, you'll understand the variations in paper, what makes a first edition, and the quality of binders and artists. You'll learn odd facts. A rare edition of a Charles Dickens book carried an illustration considered obscene in its day. Only a few of those can be found. The offending illustration was quickly pulled and replaced with a new one. That makes the first edition especially valuable. Novels by Anthony Trollope came out with ads in the back; these will date the edition you may be holding.

You'll learn how paper was made and why very old paper is sometimes superior to new. You'll discover the study of typography, the art of illustration, and the craft of fine binding.

Caring for Rare Books

A library of rare books may be for study rather than investment. But care for both the pricey and the mundane is identical. "Temperature, sunlight, and water are the worst enemies," Hollis says.

In the Norlin Library Special Collections room, most books are stored standing up (unless they are very large and wide) and in humidity- and temperature-controlled rooms. They're kept in the dark. Even when on display, the most exquisite books stay in the light for only brief periods. Photos are handled with white gloves. And the books are never completely opened; that will break the spine. Instead, they're lodged in book cradles.

This 1450s' leaf from a Gutenberg Bible is in the Norlin Library at U.C. Boulder.

When it comes to everyday book collections, book technician Kris McCusker says to avoid two typical storage areas: basements and attics, places where you'll likely find heat and humidity. And don't crowd the books, give each plenty of room.

Carol says she has loved beautifully made books since she was a teenager, eagerly searching for information on book design from 1929 onward. While these books generally go up in value, there's no guarantee that they will. She always assumes collecting books to be a passion above all else. "Many of the collectors who come to me know their books. They'll tell me they've wanted a certain book for years, but only now can afford it. In my area of fine press, you collect because you love the craftsmanship."

RESOURCES

■ COLORADO MEMBERS OF THE ANTIQUARIAN BOOKSELLER'S ASSOCIATION OF AMERICA

Chessler Books, 29723 Troutdale Scenic Drive, Evergreen, 80437; 303-670-0093; www.chesslerbooks.com. Michael Chessler specializes in mountaineering and climbing books, both new and out-of-print.

Four Rivers Books, 7228 Four Rivers Road, Boulder, 80301; 303-530-7567; www.fourriversbooks.com. Carol P. Grossman specializes in fine and private press books, artist's books, limited editions, books on books.

The Hermitage Bookshop, 290 Fillmore Street, Denver, 80206; 303-388-6811; http://bookmarque.net/HermitageBooks. The Hermitage specializes in western, first editions, women's studies, military history.

Old Algonquin Books is an Internet-only store. They specialize in first edition fiction books from the 1800s to present day, with a good selection of mysteries. They can be reached by phone, 303-431-7072 or website is: www.oldalgonquin.com.

■ DEALERS WITH ANTIQUARIAN BOOKS

Art Source International, 1237 Pearl Street, Boulder, 80302; 303-444-4079; www.rare-maps.com. Medieval manuscripts.

Sunnybank Books, Antique Gallery, 5501 South Broadway, Littleton, 80121; 303-571-1190.

■ HELPFUL ORGANIZATIONS

The American Alpine Club has a rare book collection of mountaineering and rock climbing—some books date to the 16th century. The library is open to members only. It's at 710 Tenth Street, Suite 15, Golden, 80401; 303-384-0112; www.americanalpineclub.org.

Colorado Preservation Alliance, Colorado State Archives, 1313 Sherman Street, Denver, 80203; 303-275-2214; www.archives.state.cous/cpa. Explains how to save, restore, and preserve documents.

Guild of Book Workers, 521 Fifth Avenue, New York, New York, 10175; http://palimpsest.stanford.edu/byorg/gbw.

Heritage Gateway to Colorado's Digitalization Projects; http://cdpheritage.org. Site includes Colorado archives, historical societies, libraries, and museums.

Special Collections, University of Colorado, 184 UCB, Boulder, 80309; 303-492-6144; www.libraries.colorado.edu/ps/spc/frontpage.htm.

RECOMMENDED READING

Used and Rare: Travels in the Book World by Lawrence and Nancy Goldstone (St. Martin's Press, 1997).

Slightly Chipped: Footnotes in Booklore by Lawrence and Nancy Goldstone (St. Martin's Press, 1999).

Gentle Madness: Bibliophiles, Bibliomanes, and the Eternal Passion for Books by Nicholas A. Basbanes (Henry Holt and Co.,1995).

Patience & Fortitude: A Roving Chronicle of Book People, Book Places, and Book Culture by Nicholas A. Basbanes (HarperCollins, 2001).

A Passion for Books: A Book Lover's Treasury of Stories, Essays, Humor, Lore, and Lists on Collecting, Reading, Borrowing, Lending, Caring for, and Appreciating Books, edited by Harold Rabinowitz and Rob Kaplan (Times Books, 1999).

AN ARTFUL SCIENCE: BOTANICAL PRINTS

by NIKI HAYDEN

Leaf through a collection of eighteenth- and nineteenth-century botanical prints, and you'll journey through a garden of delights. Scarlet, ruffled roses. Crisp, organza-thin anemones. White wild roses perch on slender green tendrils. Hummingbirds flash gilded heads. Raccoons—each hair tinged delicately in ochre and black—sport rascally expressions.

If you go back in time, botanical representations date to ancient Roman mosaics, says modern-day illustrator Angela Overy. Depicting the natural world gained momentum during the Middle Ages with herbals, which monks illustrated to identify medicinal plants. Throughout the Renaissance, the twin virtues of art and science consumed Leonardo da Vinci and master printer Albrecht Dürer.

Along came Carolus Linnaeus, who, in 1753, published *Species of Plants,* which established a plant classification system. He inspired entrepreneurs like Dr. Robert John Thornton, who published books of botanical prints meant to astonish the public, although his *Temple of Flora* landed him in debtors' prison. The Denver Botanic Gardens owns a copy of his famous illustrated book.

Napoleon Bonaparte bestowed gifts of botanical prints by Pierre-Joseph Redouté on visiting dignitaries. The roses from Josephine Bonaparte's garden, elegantly revealing the advancement of French botany, married science and beauty—suitable for conveying the prestige

"Red Rose" by Basil Besler.

of her husband's powerful state. John James Audubon, who attributed noble, silly, or devious characteristics to many wild animals, had become famous in America when he printed his animal illustrations in book form. Finally, in the nineteenth century, the passion for natural science unleashed by Charles Darwin led to a flurry of magazines and books filled with botanical wonders.

Prints Flourished in the Nineteenth Century

"It was a democratic art form," says Tam O'Neill, who buys and sells antique prints at her gallery in Denver. Prints reached their zenith in the nineteenth century with the rise of the middle class. And while botanical painters and printers never achieved the star status of other artists, their work appealed to scientists, naturalists, and, eventually, gardeners.

Johann Weinman lends fine detail to a clematis flower.

"I think the best botanic illustrations are scientifically correct but aesthetically pleasing," says Victoria Matthews, a botanist who is also a horticultural editor. Victoria first began purchasing watercolor paintings from young artists just getting a start in the profession. She loves botanical paintings and prints, but concedes that few considered the niche of botanical art important. Only recently has the art received much notice with major collectors. Those who prize botanical watercolors and prints are a small, select group who fill their homes with impressions of the natural world.

"I think there's a certain attraction to bringing elements of history and nature into your home," Tam says. "Life is so fast and electronic and stressful. Botanical prints are calming and centering. I find people in the sciences are responsive to them. They feel a kinship, and it's not like you have to take an art history course to get it."

John James Audubon gives his raccoon a rascally expression.

Instead of art history, you'll be wiser to take a botany class, because lovers of botanical prints prize the realism, the attention to factual accuracy, and the scientific knowledge of the artist.

Where Art and Science Meet

That's even truer today, as contemporary botanical artists research not only the plants but also their environments. "It's very important to me to include the pollinators," Angela says, because botanical art remains committed to the study of botany.

In earlier eras, she believes scientific realism replaced other, more hidden motives. The attention to the anatomy of flowers substituted in the Victorian Age for frank talk about sex. "It was acceptable for people to talk about the sexual parts of plants in ways they could not talk about people. So there were some excellent women artists who began to talk about it and be interested in it," she says.

Of course, flowers and plants appear in paintings as major subjects. Georgia O'Keeffe unveiled flowers as the star performers in her oils. And the Dutch masters spared no effort to duplicate tulips with a photographic sensibility. But botanical watercolorists and printers worked within strictures and still do today. While photography is now an essential ingredient in botany study, it hasn't diminished what the botanical print can do.

"If you have a photograph, it's the light telling the story," Angela says. "You have to use both photos and drawings to get the form and color and the scientific story that you are telling. It's acceptable to paint how you feel about that flower, but you also have to capture some of the charm and charisma. Inevitably, a little of yourself comes out."

"Publishing has tended to go through a phase of just using photographs, and more recently a trend has been to return to actual watercolor illustration," Victoria adds. Only illustrations and prints truly show the fine details of a plant as well as its growth. Scientists point out that the progression of development in the life cycle of a flower is unexcelled in illustrations and prints.

"Bird with a Gilded Head" by John Gould.

Revival in Illustration

But there's a good reason why the popularity of prints and illustrations lagged in the twentieth century. Fewer art students were interested in learning to draw realistically when the art world embraced abstraction. Scientific drawing was fostered, or perhaps reluctantly accepted, by departments of botany. The number of artists dwindled, and nearly all, Victoria says, were women, because a career in botanical illustration was generally low paying and sponsored by magazines.

Today, it's the attention to detail and realism that contributes to the popularity of antique prints. After all, you'll journey to a time when illustration reigned. But, like the plants themselves, prints have an ephemeral life. An essential ingredient to collecting botanical watercolors and prints is learning how to care for them. Watercolor is famous for fading. And prints will fade under bright light. Science has found solutions to several of these problems, such as chemicals that will

Fruits were as popular as flowers when it came to botanical scrutiny.

restore color, but it pays to learn how to conserve these fine works.

Caring for Prints and Illustrations

Special framing and archival glass will screen out some of the harm in light rays. Acid-free paper used in framing is important, and the work should be kept away from humidity. "If you have an old piece of paper, it is important to know what's been done to it," Tam says. "You need to know what was intended to be hand colored and what was not. There's a fine line [between] restoring something and making it different. If the framing isn't recent, you should take a look at the glazing and the matting. Sometimes just spending ten dollars on a new matte board will make the difference between preserving the color or not."

Purchasing an antique collection requires research. Some reproductions are sold as originals. And Angela says she has seen original plates used on new paper, but sold as original prints. A good place to begin your study is at the Denver Botanic Gardens library, as well as with print dealers who can authenticate work.

John Elwes depicts a white lily.

Lovers of science and gardening surely will take note that the notion of paradise as a garden is universal. Whether you're a scientist,

A single page from Dr. Robert John Thornton's book *Temple of Flora* reveals botany in a dramatic setting.

nature lover, or gardener, you'll find a common thread links the worlds of science and art. "I think it's an empathy with plants in general," Angela says. "Every week I find out something new, just studying them in an analytical way, much in the way people enjoy their cats or dogs. Perhaps it's because we are so far removed in our hectic lives from so much that is animated and living. So this is a connection with the world that we find."

(Photographs of prints courtesy of Tam O'Neill Fine Arts.)

RESOURCES

GALLERIES FOR BOTANICALS

Art Source International, 1237 Pearl Street, 80302; 303-444-4079; www.rare-maps.com. Antique prints including botanicals, wildlife, and maps

The Map and Botanical Gallery, 2426 East 3rd Avenue, Denver, 80206; 303-321-3676; www.oldantiquemapsandprints.com. Wide selection of botanical prints.

Mary Williams Fine Arts, 2116 Pearl Street, Boulder, 80302; 303-938-1588; www.thegreatartdoors.com. Botanicals and western.

Tam O'Neill Fine Arts, 311 Detroit Street, Denver, 80206; 1-800-428-3826; www.tamoneillfinearts.com.

HELPFUL ORGANIZATIONS

American Historical Print Collectors Society, P.O. Box 201, Fairfield, Connecticut 06824; www.ahpcs.org.

American Society of Botanical Artists, 47 Fifth Avenue, New York, New York 10003; 866-691-9080; http://huntbot.andrew.cmu.edu/ASBA/ASBotArtists.html.

Guild of Natural Science Illustrators, P.O. Box 652, Ben Franklin Station, Washington, D.C. 20044; 301-309-1514; www.gnsi.org.

Rocky Mountain Society of Botanical Artists; for information contact Kathy Imel at kjimel@aol.com, or go to www.botanicalartists.org. Meets quarterly.

MAJOR COLLECTIONS AND LIBRARIES

Hunt Institute for Botanical Documentation, 5000 Forbes Avenue, Pittsburgh, Pennsylvania 15213; 412-268-2434; http://huntbot.andrew.cmu.edu. A major center for botanical illustration.

National Agricultural Library, 10301 Baltimore Avenue, Beltsville, Maryland 20705; 301-504-5755; www.nal.usda.gov.

Temple of Flora by Dr. Robert John Thornton (self-published, 1812). Denver Botanic Gardens, 1005 York Street, Denver, 80206; 720-865-3500; www.botanicgardens.org. Several books are available on the prints of Pierre-Joseph Redouté and Thornton's *Temple of Flora*. Also, check out botanic illustration courses at the Denver Botanic Gardens.

RECOMMENDED READING

The Art of Botanical Illustration by Wilfred Blunt (Collins, 1967).

Contemporary Botanical Artists: The Shirley Sherwood Collection by Shirley Sherwood, edited by Victoria Matthews (Weidenfeld & Nicolson Ltd., 1996).

Great Flower Books, 1700–1900 by Sacheverell Sitwell and others (Atlantic Monthly Press, 1990).

A Guide to the Collecting and Care of Original Prints by Carl Zigrosser and Christa M. Gaehde (Crown Publishers, 1965).

How Prints Look by W. M. Ivins Jr. (Beacon Press, 1958).

Nature into Art by Handasyde Buchanan (Weidenfeld & Nicolson, 1979).

A Passion for Plants: Contemporary Botanical Masterworks by Shirley Sherwood (Cassell & Co., 2001).

Sex in Your Garden by Angela Overy (Fulcrum Publishing, 1997).

■ Oriental Rugs: Contemporary Designs from Nomadic Art

by NIKI HAYDEN

Chuck Paterson's Oriental carpet showroom is a windowless warehouse. Rolled, stacked, hung on walls, draped over tables—the inventory is not meant for the public because Chuck sells wholesale to shops and dealers. Here, in an organized jumble, the old and new lie side by side. A stack of nineteenth-century kilims from the Caucasus in soft reds and indigo blues shares space with newly knotted rugs in modern geometric designs from Turkey. The first is the product of rural life in the rugged countryside of Azerbaijan, the second a commercial rug-making workshop in Turkey catering to American designer trends. Each pile represents a chapter in the contemporary history of Oriental rugs.

A late nineteenth-century hand-knotted rug is from the border area between Afghanistan and Iran.

Antiques Vie with New

Oriental rugs were prized in colonial America and featured in the paintings of the Dutch in the 1700s. But history determines the available carpets. Throughout the 1990s, a deluge of antique rugs surfaced in the world market after the collapse of the Soviet Union. Most appeared as relinquished heirlooms from homes in Central Asia. At the same time, cottage industries mushroomed in countries like Turkey, Iran, and Pakistan, which also provide hand-knotted and woven rugs suited for contemporary tastes and destined for the world carpet market.

A hand-knotted recent designed by Tolga Tollu in Turkey.

Chuck imports both. His expertise lies in Caucasus textiles, the major folk art of villages isolated by two giant mountain chains—the highest in Europe—which cradle the republics of Georgia, Armenia, and Azerbaijan, as well as the south of Russia. Each shares a tangled history of invasions, religious wars, oppression, and terrorism—sometimes against each other. Despite their conflicts, they share similar industries, and hand-woven rugs remain an important commodity.

"When the Soviet Union fell apart," Chuck says, "areas of Central Asia became independent for the first time in sixty years. The true financial poverty of the people came to light. There was a mass grab for power by those who had influence. The quality of life for most of the people went down, and they began to sell off their heirlooms. Nobody in the West knew how many antique kilims these people had. They began selling off jewelry, paintings, and rugs. That has fed the market for the last ten years. It's just now coming to an end. It has been both interesting and sad to watch."

At the same time, immigrants from these new republics flooded into the United States, uniting with family members. And many brought rugs with them. One of the largest Armenian American communities, situated in Los Angeles, welcomed relatives who arrived with rugs rolled up and stuffed in suitcases. "Typically, the immigrants would have an uncle or cousin who is in the rug business and they would become a contact," setting the new arrival up as an importer from the old country, Chuck says. Armenian American families have been involved in much of the rug trade throughout the twentieth century.

Where Markets Flourish

Chuck's interest in Oriental rugs dates to 1982 when he first noticed a rug in a Boston store window. He stood outside gazing intently until the shop owner introduced himself and invited Chuck in. What began as a chance encounter with a carpet importer who later became a mentor has developed into a career. Chuck travels throughout Europe assessing and gathering Oriental weavings, flocking to the major cities where importers and exporters congregate.

Detail from a 1920s flat hand-woven Azerbaijan rug or tapestry.

"New York is a capital for the American market, increasingly used by high-level dealers who bring expensive things there. London is also a major source, primarily of antique rugs, which are popular all throughout Europe. Germany also is a destination," Chuck says, but his interests lie elsewhere.

"Istanbul is my major source. It's mixed. Most new production is in Turkey, but you can also find the old from Central Asia—Uzbekistan, Turkmenistan, the Caucasus. Because it's an Islamic country, many of the rug merchants from those countries feel comfortable there. Turkey is in a unique position between Europe and Central Asia. It's also very friendly toward Americans and tourists."

Origins Lie in Nomadic Past

The region, or latitude, of great rug making, a kind of textile band, stretches from Turkey to India. The reason, Chuck says, can be summed up in one word: *sheep.* In mountainous terrain, sheep are a staple crop, and cultures in the Caucasus and Central Asia developed textiles with elaborate designs to serve as bedding, wall insulation, and tent coverings. Easy to roll up and transport, rugs point to an ancient nomadic way of life as well as a division of labor. Women spin and weave; men shear and dye.

Rugs of the region are constructed with a sturdy row of double-plied yarn stretched on a wooden frame. The softer dyed weft is woven over and under the vertical warp. If tiny knots are looped, they are locked in place by the soft weft. Weaving is a universal and timeless invention that has been used throughout the world for a thousand years or more. What sets Oriental rugs apart from those created by other rug-making cultures is their elaborate designs, and, although they may have been woven as bedding, they contain a coarse sheep's wool or goat hair that ensures a long life of wear. "These were rug techniques that go back a millennium," Chuck says, "and had to serve multiple purposes."

As beautiful as they might be, Chuck says that rugs over one hundred years old may not fit modern designer trends. They don't come in the most popular sizes. That's because they were woven for a family in Armenia and not America. A collector will prize the natural dyes of madder root, cochineal, and indigo as well as the intricate design. But contemporary tastes dictate to the weaver now, not the village tradition. "The lack of color, a desire for neutrals, is very

Close-up border of an Azerbaijan flat hand-woven rug or tapestry.

different from the traditional colors," Chuck says, "but that is what the western designers want for homes."

Techniques Transfer to Modern Design

Most fans of these intricately designed rugs point to the instinctive color harmonies and intricate embellishment as profoundly Central Asian in aesthetic. We've been told that ancient Islamic designs never depicted the natural forms of people or animals. These were reminders of banned pre-Islamic societies whose gods once were rendered in drawings and sculptures.

But Chuck says the intent was never so rigid. He finds that some designs, even traditional rugs, evoke natural forms—like a bird in a tree. Designs could be flexible, and rugs today, as impeccably handwoven as those in the nineteenth century, are created in pale colors with European motifs. Whether abstract or naturalistic, the leap from village design to contemporary abstraction has taken place. New designs vie for popularity with the old.

Recent hand-knotted rug designed by Tolga Tollu in Turkey.

A Turkish architect-turned-rug designer operates his own rug workshop, turning out designs with a modern touch. Tolga Tollu lives in Istanbul. His German-born wife markets the abstract painterly compositions that relate more closely to the New York school of abstract impressionism than to traditional Turkish emblems. Rugs are now international in appearance, even if the techniques are ancient.

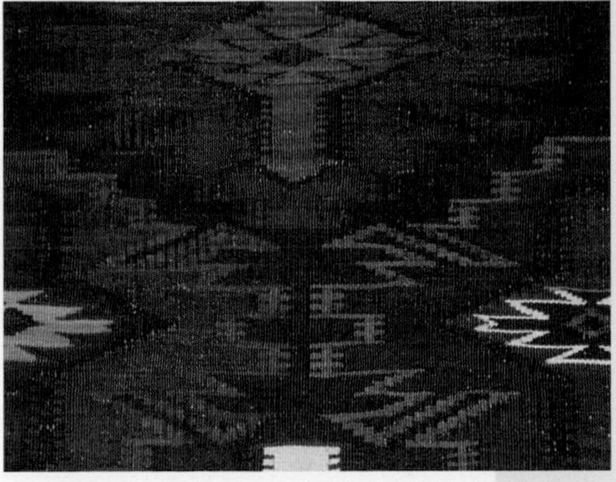

A detail from a nineteenth-century flat hand-woven tapestry from Azerbaijan.

Chuck's antique rugs are folded along one wall. They're crisp and clean, washed with a mild soap and water. A high quality rug won't have colors that run, and Chuck doesn't recommend dry-cleaning antique kilims. But the flat, lovely kilims are less popular today than the newer pile carpeting. Pile carpets will withstand more wear; that accounts for their dominance in the carpet market. A kilim can be used on the floor, but only with special care. They never were intended for foot traffic.

Advice for Potential Collectors

A few village names are synonymous with outstanding rugs: Bijar and Sultanabad from Iran are considered among the finest. But Chuck suggests novices visit as many rug dealers as they can. And if you intend to buy more than one, develop a relationship with a dealer who has been in the business for a long time and carries a sterling reputation.

"Buy the best that you can afford," he says. "In antique rugs, if you have bought one that is reasonably priced, it won't go down in value. Stick with someone who has been in the business for a while and whose focus is Oriental rugs." Most buyers, he says, can't judge the quality of workmanship and must rely on information given by a reputable dealer.

It's common practice now to allow prospective buyers to take a rug home for a day or two and move it from room to room or under varied lighting. Oriental rugs are colorful, which means they will often dominate a room. Carpet dealers will want you to be happy with your purchase and give ample opportunity for you to try one out.

The huge revival in rug weaving throughout Central Asia in the last fifteen years has altered designs to such a degree that Chuck says "the nomadic weaver would never understand. None of these new rugs would have looked like this one hundred years ago." He balks at choosing a favorite kilim or region. Buying kilims is more complex than any single ethnic group or design. Instead, he says the most beautiful carpets come from historical periods of stability and peace. "When life was good, what they made came up to a very high standard. When I look for old pieces, I look for serenity. That is reflected in the hand of the maker. When life was harder, the production went into a decline."

RESOURCES

■ HELPFUL ORGANIZATION

Colorado Textile Group; contact Richard Stewart at 303-444-3720.

■ SPECIALTY BOOK DEALERS

Marla Mallett Textiles, 1690 Johnson Road NE, Atlanta, Georgia 30306; 404-872-3356; www.marlamallett.com. Contains detail about books, organizations, history, links to textile resources and online sales.

Myrna Bloom, The East–West Room, 3139 Alpin Drive, Dresher, Pennsylvania 19025; 215-657-0178; www.myrnabloom.com. A virtual bookstore specializing in carpet and textile books.

■ REGIONAL DEALERS

Art Bank, 610 North Tejon Street, Colorado Springs, 80903; 719-634-6073. Hand-knotted rugs.

Azari Rug Gallery, 1410 South Broadway, Denver, 80210; 303-744-2222; www.azari-rug.com. Persian and Oriental rugs.

BlueCrate, 335 West Main Street, Trinidad, 81082; 719-846-4077; www.bluecrate.net. Tibetan hand-knotted wool carpets.

Cherry Creek Oriental Rugs, 3200 East Third Avenue, Denver, 80206; 303-333-4040.

Kimbulian & Noury Oriental Rugs, 126 Acoma Street, Denver, 80223; 303-744-1858. Primarily cleaning and restoration.

Lilihan Oriental Rugs, 2486 South Colorado Boulevard, Denver, 80222; 303-691-6900.

Oriental & Navajo Rug Co., 929 Main Street, Longmont, 80501; 303-772-7962; www.orientalandnavajorugs.com.

Robert Mann Oriental Rugs, 2540 Walnut Street, Denver, 80205; 303-292-2522. Antique rugs and expert cleaning services.

Sarkisian's Oriental Rugs, 693 East Speer Boulevard, Denver, 80203; 303-733-2623; www.sarkisian.com.

Shaver–Ramsey Oriental Rugs & Accents, 2414 East Third Avenue, Denver, 80206; 303-320-6363; www.shaver-ramsey.com.

■ RECOMMENDED READING

Cloudband; www.cloudband.com. An online magazine specializing in carpets and textiles. Includes online auctions similar to eBay.

Hali; www.hali.com. A beautiful magazine that caters to rug collectors, dealers, museums; with lavish photos and scholarly articles.

Country Furniture: Village Cabinetmakers Craft a Style Fit for Kings

by CAROL WARD

In seventeenth- and eighteenth-century Europe, ornately carved and veneered furniture may have been crafted in the courts of the French kings, but village cabinetmakers took note of the details. They made their own interpretations simpler and more appropriate to country living. Rather than expensive imported mahogany, everyday tables, chairs, and cupboards were made of local pine, oak, and cherry. Country furniture originated as farm versions of royal grandeur, spreading throughout the French provinces of Brittany, Normandy and Provence, Germany's Black Forest, Swedish villages, and even England.

Houses were small, and farm folk didn't need and couldn't afford a lot of furniture. Ordinary people were too busy surviving from day to day, so they had the requisite table and chairs and a few other practical pieces. Charm was born from necessity. For modern collectors, basic needs haven't changed, either.

A detail from a French armoire now used as a bookcase.

Suzanne MacKenzie, owner of Stuart–Buchanan Ltd. in Denver, carries early–eighteenth-century to mid–nineteenth-century European country furniture. "Functional furniture is what people want to invest in," Suzanne says. "My best-selling pieces are farm tables, buffets, side tables, and armoires." Having developed her collector's eye at the Leslie Hindman Auction House in Chicago, Suzanne visits the French countryside several times a year. She scouts for pieces at regional fairs, vendors, and even at the

Paris Flea Market, where she discovered a wonderful country armoire.

A close-up of the armoire carving reveals that it was a marriage gift.

Armoires, Tables, and Chairs: The Basic Stock of Country

Country homes consisted of one or two rooms with all the family living under one roof. With no closets or storage spaces, armoires housed the family's linens and other personal items. Because of its large size, an armoire could provide much-needed privacy. Armoires remain in relatively good condition because they were the cherished centerpieces of the house. And like many Europeans, the French stayed in the same house generation after generation, passing on pieces through the family. Only rarely were they buffeted by the wear and tear of moving.

Some armoires were carved simply, while others feature grand detail. The more elaborate were usually marriage armoires—those that were commissioned as a wedding gift—rich with carvings symbolic of the couple's union, perhaps a cornucopia filled with an abundance of fruits and flowers or two lovebirds.

Armoires have adapted to changed times. Large narrow marriage armoires sometimes took on a second life as an impressive *bibliothèque*—a library or bookcase. And while some are much too large for many of today's homes, "People like the smaller armoires and use them for their bedrooms, guest rooms, and second homes. They make great television and entertainment centers," Suzanne says.

When it comes to good condition, armoires are the exception. Most country furniture was practical rather than decorative—for cooking, slaughtering livestock, mending. That some of it has survived is testimony to how well it was made but also explains the nicks and scratches. Tables, of course, were the most heavily used of all. "A table might be put in a cold barn, rather than discarded, to sit on icy cold floors for years and years. So the feet have to be replaced and repainted to match," Suzanne says. "Country furniture is in a different category than other antiques. These pieces require work to get them back to their original condition."

Although tables can be restored, chairs often cannot. Quality reproductions seem to be preferred to most chairs that do survive. "People don't want to sit on a small rickety chair," Suzanne says. "If the chair has a strong construction and is made of a hardy wood such as ash, it will last two to three generations. Even people who have a passion for antiques will end up with a set of reproduction chairs."

Her English ladder-back chairs are based on the regional Lincolnshire chair. A typical price for a dining chair is $700, for an armchair, $1,000. Rush, a type of grass, is rarely used today. Instead, reproduction chairs are made with a strong paper product, which looks very much the same as rush but is less expensive.

This English ladder-back chair is a reproduction. Chairs are among the most fragile of country pieces.

Our contemporary tastes rely on upholstered furniture and ample storage space in a home's recesses, but benches and blanket chests served those purposes in the eighteenth and nineteenth centuries. A circa 1810 English oak bench in the style of George I, with turnings, heavy stretchers, carved paneling, and in its original state, lines a wall. Benches of this sort are practical as well as interesting in the entryway, hallway, or foyer. Cushions soften their austere appearance.

An early–nineteenth-century French blanket chest still is used for storage. At a distance it gives the appearance of a painted piece. Only on closer inspection do you see the amazing artistry of the cabinetmaker, who may have been showing off his skill. The chest, with its exceptional design, is detailed with a fruitwood inlay and brass tacks. Placing it at the end of a bed makes it a showpiece—and a rare item. Typical of northern Brittany, country furniture from this area has become difficult to find.

A sturdy nineteenth-century French blanket chest is put to its original use—storage.

Similar to the English rack and dresser, a cherry wood *vaisselier,* a cupboard with plate guards, is unique to the French countryside. One, found in the southern Loire region, has an arched top; three shelves over two drawers and two doors. Its inlaid star is an old and common symbol on furniture throughout the Loire countryside. In Provence, the star would be replaced with the urn—a mark of the region's water identity. Sail to England and you'll find furniture that reflects a different national love—dogs. An 1860 English pine "dog kennel" sideboard with dresser base, six drawers flanking one drawer, was made without the bottom center door so that dogs could go in, curl up, and nest in its nook.

Germans and Scandinavians Loved Painted Wood

Pine is plentiful in the German forests, and the German cabinetmakers loved to paint, rather than carve, their country furniture. A regional piece, made about 1830, from the Black Forest, with painted floral panels over two doors and one bottom drawer, is in its nearly original state. (Usually the feet are replaced.) It was obviously a prized possession and meant to be the focal point in the family home. "It's incredible how well the paint has been retained over the years," Suzanne says.

Then, too, there was a practical reason to paint. Often, different kinds of woods were used to make a piece of furniture. Painting it was almost necessary. Incongruent wood colors and grains looked much better covered up. Following the European tradition, this practice was popular among the Pennsylvania Dutch carpenters. Although they are called Dutch, the immigrants were Germans who migrated to the eastern region of that state, carrying out the traditions of their original home.

Many country pieces were painted with a dark dense paint. Colors were often red and pine green—the "ox-blood" red based on rust—while white and light-colored paint based on milk were used as a base. Cabinets often are in good condition because they've been cared for over the years, so the urge to fix scratched or marred areas should be weighed carefully. Furniture that has been stripped or repainted may lose value. "You should leave a piece alone if the original finish is on it and it looks great. Another piece of advice is to never refinish a piece yourself—"Get a professional," Suzanne says.

A panel from a German chest painted in earthy colors.

Painted furniture in Sweden and other Scandinavian countries was so popular that it's not uncommon to find Swedish furniture that has been painted over by second and third generations. And a unique subculture of painters in Sweden specialized in grain painting. These painters could make lesser woods look like the grains of richer woods. A plain pine bench takes on the look of a burled wood, birch, or mahogany. While different from painting a design on a piece of furniture, it was yet another interpretation of how to copy a city style to fit country needs and pocketbooks.

Country European Influences in America

The British influenced colonial America, but all immigrants brought traditions from their countries of origin. In the English home you would likely find a Windsor chair. The German and Dutch families brought large cupboards and wardrobes. And there were the traveling pieces, such as blanket chests, that carried belongings and the prized family china.

The French cupboard with plate guards is from the Loire region.

Unlike the Europeans, Americans were on the move from the beginning, either by design or necessity. Table legs could be detached from the table's top. Breakaway wardrobes were quickly disassembled. If Americans were relocating, their furniture was going with them. Later, the nineteenth century brought new industrial techniques in production. Furniture made in the factory was more accessible to the public. The costly handmade mixed with cheaper factory items.

Americans are still on the move. And, most of us can't afford a home full of period pieces. But many of us can have one or two period pieces mixed with reproductions, if so desired, along with today's furniture. "You don't have to have a lot of antiques," says Suzanne. "If you have a fabulous antique rug and a few antiques and mix it in with a great sofa and a couple contemporary pieces, you will achieve a look that you want."

She advises people to look for pieces that have multiple functions. Smaller, less expensive pieces that have many uses, such as a blanket chest, can be used for storage, seating, or a coffee table. Then, consider dining room furniture, which, Suzanne notes, "will last forever and be passed down to your children. But always go for the best quality that you can afford and go slowly." Shifting her focus away from expensive case pieces such as armoires, when the economy is unpredictable, Suzanne suggests side tables: "A side table is the perfect period piece to purchase without making a huge investment."

Accessories: It's All in the Details

For those of us who truly desire the real thing, Suzanne points to accessories such as old baskets, faience (tin-glazed earthenware), and mirrors. "Everyone needs a mirror," Suzanne says, pointing to an antique Spanish mirror hanging in a quiet corner. On closer inspection, the faded painting on the mirror frame depicting a Spanish scene reveals touches of Moorish influence.

A uniquely French decorative touch is the confit pot. Confit pots are ceramic pots that stored duck fat. The fat was used for cooking and food preservation. Painted with a brilliant glaze, usually yellow, the pot would be buried halfway into the ground to keep the fat warm and pliable. The bottom half of the pot would return to its original earthenware color, while the yellow glaze remained on the upper half. Typical large confit pots may cost $375; smaller pots are less costly. Although yellow was the common color, you may see some with a rare green glaze.

Confit pots are ceramic pots used for storage and painted in vivid colors.

While confit pots are indeed fascinating, the old standbys are just as exciting. The English country home with chintz reached its pinnacle in the eighteenth century. There were few sofas and chairs that weren't covered with faded flowered English chintz. But you don't have to wait years for the softened colors; there are fabric companies today that will sell it to you already faded. Soaking fabric in tea (not herbal teas—only those with tannic acid) will do the job, too.

In France, the reigning fabric was toile de Jouy. Toile, meaning cloth or canvas, was made in the village Jouy-en-Josas. Located near Versailles, the townspeople enjoyed a long and steady demand for textiles from the palace and other estate homes. Later, with a new process of printing on cotton, the now-familiar blue or red pastoral and mythological scenes on a white background became more available. There are fabric companies both in France and the United States that have revived the older original patterns. Lace, French copper pots and pans, colorful Provençal prints, and fresh flowers are all great accessories.

And in your American country kitchen, accessories such as old mixing bowls and yellowware—an English and American rustic bisque and yellow pottery—and mid–twentieth-century table linens are popular. Americana is associated with colorful quilts, rag rugs, and the lingering scent of dry herbs and flowers hanging from ceiling hooks. Old family photos, personal collections, pie safes, and anything Shaker qualifies as American country. But also consider the furniture that has been handed down to you, or discovered at antiques shows, shops, garage and estate sales, and flea markets. Country is not a style, but more a trend to embrace a casual elegance that celebrates the ordinary and everyday designs so well used for generations.

RESOURCES

ANTIQUE DISTRICT

Denver Antique Row, 400–1800 South Broadway (and 25–27 East Dakota Avenue), Denver, 80210; 303-733-5251; www.antiques-colorado.com/antiquerow.

EUROPEAN AND WORLD

Another Time, Another Place, 1181 South Street, Louisville, 80027; 720-890-7700; www.atapantiques.com. French.

The Apiary, 585 Milwaukee Street, Denver, 80206; 303-399-6017.

Black Tulip Antiques Ltd., 1370 South Broadway, Denver, 80210; 303-777-1370.

Ca Shi, 3458 Walnut Street, Denver, 80205; 303-297-2947. Asian.

DjUNA, 221 Detroit Street, Denver, 80206; 303-355-3500. Eclectic.

East–West Designs, 303 Josephine Street, Denver, 80206; 303-316-9520. Japanese.

Eron Johnson Antiques, Ltd., 451 Broadway, Denver, 80203; 303-777-8700. World.

Indochine, 2525 Arapahoe Avenue, Boulder, 80302; 303-444-7734. Asian.

McKinley & Hill Antiques, 4340 Harlan Street, Wheat Ridge, 80033; 303-424-1102. English, American, French.

Metropolitan Antiques Gallery, 1147 Broadway, Denver, 80203; 303-623-3333.

Paris Blue, 350 Kalamath Street, Denver, 80223; 720-932-6200.

Shaggy Ram, 0210 Edwards Village Boulevard, P.O. Box 2727, Edwards, 81632; 970-926-7377. French, English.

Sheilagh Malo Antiques, 1211 East Fourth Avenue, Denver, 80206; 303-777-3418.

Stuart–Buchanan Antiques Ltd., 1530 Fifteenth Street, Denver, 80202; 303-825-1222. Country European.

Warner's Antiques, 1401 South Broadway, Denver, 80210; 303-722-9173; www.warnersantiques.com. Asian, European, American.

■ EARLY AMERICAN

John Boulware Antiques, 1416 South Broadway, Denver, 80210; 303-733-7369.

Starr Antiques, 2940 East Sixth Avenue, Denver, 80206; 303-399-4537.

■ RUSTIC AND MOUNTAIN

Little Bear Antiques & Uniques, 415 South Spring Street, Aspen, 81611; 970-925-3705.

Shepton's Antiques, 389 South Broadway, Denver, 80209; 303-777-5115. Rustic teak, pine, architectural.

Ski Country Antiques, 114 Homestead Road, Evergreen, 80439; 303-674-4666.

■ AMERICAN EARLY TWENTIETH CENTURY

Antique Legacy, 2624 West Colorado Avenue, Colorado Springs, 80904; 719-578-0637.

Antiques at Lincoln Park, 822 Eighth Street, Greeley, 80631; 970-351-6222.

Bennett Antiques, 1220 South College Avenue, Fort Collins, 80524; 970-482-3645; www.bennettantiques.com.

Brass Armadillo, Antique Mall, 11301 West I-70 Frontage Road, Wheat Ridge, 80033; 303-403-1677.

The Collection, 899 Broadway, Denver, 80203; 303-623-4200; www.antiquedesign.com.

Colorado Antique Gallery, 5501 South Broadway, Littleton, 80121; 303-794-8100.

Days Gone by Antiques, 356 Main Street, Longmont, 80501; 303-651-1912.

Karen's Antiques, 1415 South Broadway, Denver, 80210; 303-871-9922.

Main Street Antique Mall, 370 Main Street, Longmont, 80501; 303-776-8511.

Niwot Antiques, 136 Second Avenue, Niwot, 80544; 303-652-2587.

Off Her Rocker Antiques, 4 East First Street, Nederland, 80466; 303-258-7976.

Old Century Antiques, 1202 West Colorado Avenue, Colorado Springs, 80904; 719-633-3439.

A Quartermoon Market, 315 East Pikes Peak Avenue, Colorado Springs, 80903; 719-633-3999.

Ralston Brothers Antiques, 425 High Street, Lyons, 80540; 303-823-6982.

Twiggs, 165 Second Avenue, Niwot, 80544; 303-652-9065.

■ TOILE, CHINTZ, FABRICS

Calico Corners, 252 Clayton Street, Denver, 80206; 303-377-7055. Lots of Toile. Books to order chintz.

Denver Fabrics, Inc., 2777 West Belleview Avenue, Littleton, 80123; 303-730-2777; www.denverfabrics.com. Lots of toile. Books to order chintz.

Elfriede's Fine Fabrics & Studio Bernina, 2460 Canyon Boulevard, Boulder, 80302; 303-447-0132. Carries toile but not chintz.

Home Decorator Fabrics, 8230 South Colorado Boulevard, Littleton, 80122; 303-779-2573. Lots of toile. Books to order chintz.

Depression Cheer

A Touch of Glass: Gift of the Great Depression

by CAROL WARD

Glass was never high on my list of collectibles—I'm a lover of pottery, antique jewelry, and well, yes, other stuff. But I recently attended my first depression-era glass show. The show was held in Denver in a banquet room of a local hotel. After waiting in line to get in and having my hand stamped at the door, I stepped into the hall and immediately felt what a small child must feel upon entering Disneyland for the first time.

Depression-era glass was well made, lustrous, and original—often as a give-away with products such as soap powder.

I looked out into a sea of glass—beautiful gleaming glass in an array of colors—green, pink, blue, lavender, and yellow. All in so many different patterns, which I would learn more about later—dishes, bowls, cups and saucers, platters, wine goblets, decanters, even candlesticks and lamps. The patterns had names like Oyster & Pearl, Raindrops, Horseshoe, Thumbprint, Starlight, and Miss America.

The crowd was enormous—so many women *and* men. I was surprised by the number of men. Some were doing the obligatory escorting, but a third looked to be serious glass fans. I chuckled about this until I found myself stuck behind a big six-footer who would not budge. He was caressing a dish. I couldn't see over him or get around him. I gave up and returned to that booth later to get a better look. Buying by all was brisk.

Jadeite is shiny, thick, opaque pale green glass that was meant to be serviceable.

Nostalgia and Aesthetics

Just what is the fascination for a glass that was primarily used as give-away pieces in the 1930s and 1940s?

Martie Grubenhoff, co-owner with her husband, Ken, of Glass Roots in Denver, and a member of the Rocky Mountain Chapter for Depression Glass, cites a couple of reasons for the popularity. "Many people remember some relative—their grandmother or aunt—who had the glass. They may have inherited some pieces and want to fill out the set. Plus the glassware was beautiful and so intricately made in that era. Glass like this is not being made today." Nostalgia and aesthetics are what it comes down to.

Depression glass came in gold, yellow, purple, blue, pink, and green.

Depression glass got its name from the Great Depression and was produced from 1929 until 1939, when World War II began. However, depression glass is defined as colored glassware mass-produced from the late 1920s through the 1940s. At depression-glass shows you will see glass made through the 1950s and 1960s. It

The simplicity of depression-era glass allows it to mix with a variety of dinnerware.

was produced by many different companies throughout the country.

Most depression glass was machine made, but there were hand-blown pieces in the elegant glassware such as Cambridge, Fostoria, Heisey, Duncan & Miller, and Tiffin glass.

Many of the dinnerware items were given away by merchants to customers using their services or buying their products. A punchbowl came with an oil change, cake plates with the purchase of flour. Pieces were buried in boxes of oatmeal and detergent. There was "dish night" at the movies, where you would get a piece of dinnerware for attending the movie. It was also sold at five-and-dime stores.

"Back then you could get salt-and-pepper shakers for five cents," Grubenhoff says. "A whole set of dishes sold for two dollars and ninety-eight cents. In the 1960s and through the 1970s you could get loads of depression glass very inexpensively." Grubenhoff recalls many Sundays coming home from flea markets with the back of her station wagon full of depression glass. Books were written about this era of glass and people started to pay attention. The popularity of the glass soared, and a bargain became harder and harder to find.

Yesterday's Bargains, Today's Treasures

Today, with the passage of time, inflation, and people's awareness of how special this glass is, prices continue to climb. However, prices vary depending upon the pattern, particular pieces, and geography.

Naturally, the more rare the piece and beloved the pattern, the more expensive. But, according to Barbara and Jim Mauzy in their book *Mauzy's*

Depression Glass (Schiffer Publishing, 2001), there are now 140 patterns recorded. That should leave many wonderful and reasonably priced pieces to collect. Find a pattern in a color you like that is in your budget (certain colors are more prized and hard to find). And when you're out and about, keep an eye open for it, because it's out there. Look everywhere. Start in your own home.

At the Denver show I purchased four pink luncheon dishes of the Old Colony pattern. Of all the patterns, this one, with its open-edge lacework, appealed to me. I checked with several dealers at the show that day and found that for the same dishes, the price was standard plus or minus a couple of dollars. The plates cost me $28 each.

Then, on a recent visit home, I asked my mother about an old bowl, which had belonged to my grandmother. And what do you think it was? A lovely pink piece of Old Colony. My mother kindly gave it to me. Now, I'll be checking thrift shops, yard sales, flea markets, and antique shops for additional pieces. Perhaps one day I'll have enough Old Colony to throw a dinner party, although my four dishes and one bowl look quite fetching mixed with my other china.

Always look for pieces in the best condition. Glass that is in less-than-mint condition, whether it is cracked, chipped, badly scratched, or poorly molded, is not desirable. Should you wish to sell, such pieces will bring very little money. When buying a piece, hold the glass up to the light (some scratching is expected, but not a lot). Run your finger around the edges. Very small chips are easy to miss by only looking at the piece.

Some stores specialize in depression-era glass, but you'll also find it tucked away on shelves in antique shops everywhere.

Also, be aware that reproductions are being made. To guard against buying anything but the real McCoy, visit shops that specialize in depression glass, and go to shows to become more familiar with your subject. Read and learn about the pieces that were made. "For example," Grubenhoff says, "the Cherry Blossom pattern children's tea set is being reproduced. But the repro tea set has a butter dish. There was no butter dish in the original depression–era Cherry Blossom child's tea set. There are a number of telltale signs with reproductions, but you must be informed."

GLASS DEFINITIONS

Blown glass—Glass shaped by air pressure

Carnival glass—Iridescent glass from the early 1900s

Cut glass—Glass cut by hand or machine into decorative patterns

Elegant glass—Handmade depression glass; finely designed and set apart from mass-marketed depression glass

Etched glass—Glass with a design cut into it

Flint glass—Glass made with silica or lead

Jadite—Opaque green glass; generally the shade of green associated with jade

Milk glass—Opaque white glass; heavy

Off-hand or free-blown—Blown glass made without a mold

Pattern glass—Glass from the late 1800s and early 1900s

Polishing—Smoothing the surface of glass with fire, chemicals, or abrasion to remove mold lines

Pontil—Mark left on a finished piece of glass after it has been snapped off the pontil (the rod used to hold the piece)

Pressed glass—Molten glass poured into a mold

Vaseline—Translucent yellow glassware similar in color to Vaseline

---

RESOURCES

DEALERS

Colorado Antique Gallery (Joseph Lucente), 5501 South Broadway, Littleton, 80121; 303-794-8100.

Glass Roots (Ken and Martie Grubenhoff), 27 East Dakota Avenue, Denver, 80209; 303-778-8693.

Harold's Collectables (Harold and Carole Keller), 6244 South Cook Drive, Centennial, 80121; www.dealersdirect.com/Dealer/Keller.

Hooked on Glass, 1407 South Broadway, Denver, 80210; 303-778-7845.

Nevada Avenue Antiques, John and Gina Sharp, 405 South Nevada Avenue, Colorado Springs, 80903; 719-473-3351.

Oil City Merchants, 126 West Main, Florence, 81226; 719-784-6582.

Ralston Brothers Antiques, Inc., 426 High Street, Lyons, 80540; 303-823-6982.

Rory & Cha's Antiques, 123 South Union Avenue, Pueblo, 81003; 719-253-0373.

HELPFUL ORGANIZATIONS

National Depression Glass Association, P.O. Box 8264, Wichita, Kansas 67208; www.ndga.net.

Rocky Mountain Depression Glass Society; http://members.aol.com/iwantglass/indexg5.html.

■ Fiesta Dinnerware: Cheerful Design in a Somber Decade

by NIKI HAYDEN

At first glance, Fiesta dinnerware appears to have sprung from the 1950s. With bright confetti colors and sleek design, perhaps it's the product of American optimism in that decade or post–World War II euphoria. Fiesta's cheerfulness is thoroughly deceiving.

Ironically, Fiesta originated during the Great Depression amid poverty, gloom, and doom. And the designer wasn't American at all, but an Englishman, Frederick Hurten Rhead, lured to American shores by a dinnerware company. Rhead designed the art deco shape, and chief engineer Albert Victor Bleininger fabricated the glazes of the vividly hued Fiesta.

Originally designed in the 1930s, colorful Fiesta still is manufactured.

With its modest 1936 price—109 pieces for $14.95 in department stores—Fiesta was handed to many a bride, and sales reached their zenith in 1937 when twelve million pieces were snapped up. Some brides accepted the gift reluctantly and stored it in the back of a cupboard.

"My mother gave it to me when I graduated from college," says Colorado collector Eleanor Crandall. "I didn't like the colors and it looked out of date at that point." Original colors included red, cobalt blue, green, yellow, and ivory. One year later, turquoise joined the group.

Nested bowls display the original colors of Fiestaware.

Fiesta Becomes a Collector's Passion

Times and tastes change. Eventually, Eleanor opened the door to her cupboard. Nested bowls looked as cheerful as a basket of dyed eggs. Eleanor had to agree with her mother: classic art deco shapes in companionable colors mix and match. No matter how humble, Fiesta made a bold design.

"It was not until 1975 that I started collecting," she says. Fiesta now is collected with passion, so much so that rare pieces are pricier and harder to find.

Eleanor's home is decorated in neutral basics: couches, rugs, and modern furniture—all in gray. It's the perfect backdrop for turquoise, yellow, green, red, and cobalt blue Fiesta. The theme extends to Mexican motif place mats and tablecloths. Shelves of Fiesta line the wall with color as brilliant international flags.

Eleanor brings out green and red Fiesta plates for the winter holidays. In the summer, turquoise and ivory keep company with yellow for a southwestern touch. Glasses are rimmed with the same festive colors. Swizzle sticks in matching hues abound.

Fiesta designers hoped a variety of colors would allow the owner to set a spirited table with affordable pieces. Did that yellow plate break just now? No matter, here's one in turquoise. Set a table in vivid colors and, as in a rainbow, they'll never clash.

Fiesta challenged the notion that all plates and cups had to match in color.

"Many, like me, started collecting to complete a set," Eleanor says. Perhaps a mother died and a set was broken up to give to each of her three grown children. "Then, you get to like it," she adds. "At first it's just one bowl, or one casserole in a different color. Then it's two of every place setting." Eleanor began to attend depression-glass shows and would discover a missing bowl or a top that fit her topless yellow sugar bowl.

A couple of rare soup bowls came her way, then a coveted twelve-inch green vase. The Homer Laughlin China Company in Newell, West Virginia, Fiesta's manufacturer, once produced candlesticks and small ornamental animals, egg cups, syrup canisters, salt-and-pepper shakers, teapots, ashtrays, ice pitchers, coffeepots, bud vases, salad bowls, relish trays, and glasses. Eleanor has them all.

Eleanor is convinced that many Fiesta collectors began their quest because it was an affordable collectible—close to its original value. The sturdy pottery was practical for everyday use, and prices never climbed to the levels of elegant depression glassware. Only recently have rare pieces commanded prices of $1,000 and up, and one piece sold for a record $10,000.

A Radioactive Scare

Besides the bright colors, Homer Laughlin made lines in gray, ivory, and black. The original and brightest color—red—was suspended during wartime because the government needed uranium oxide for a new bomb—and that led to rumors that red Fiesta might be radioactive.

According to Dave Conley, director of retail sales for Homer Laughlin, the radioactivity was not enough to be dangerous, but it was enough to register on a Geiger counter. By 1959, the glaze formula was reconfigured and red returned.

All Fiesta was discontinued from 1973 to 1986. When it was reprised, various colors appeared, only to be discontinued, such as a distinctive lilac color that made a brief appearance from 1993 to 1995.

A Classic that's Still Around

Today, Fiesta is dominated by pastels and a new blue green called Juniper. An orange called Persimmon came out in 1995, and a purplish red called Cinnabar came out in 2001. And cobalt blue, an original 1936 color, has returned to the lineup.

Fiesta is available in department stores, just as it was in 1936. And it's affordable, too, although you won't find depression prices. There are sixty different items available, and a five-piece setting is priced between $20 and $30.

"Some collectors were afraid the values of collected Fiesta would plummet when we came back in 1986," Conley says. "Instead, it just increased the interest. Today, more people are collecting the new Fiesta than the old Fiesta. Younger buyers are attracted to the colors. I think it's the art deco shape that gives it a timeless quality. Other companies came out with the colors but did it on shapes that were quickly outdated."

The date of most Fiestaware can be determined by its color.

RESOURCES

Homer Laughlin China Company, Sixth and Harrison Streets, Newell, West Virginia 26050; 800-452-4462; www.hlchina.com.

HELPFUL ORGANIZATIONS

Depression Glass MegaShow; www.glassshow.com. A source for glass, books, information.

Pike's Peak Depression Glass Club; http://members.aol.com/iwantglass/indexg2.html. Information on meetings and shows.

Rocky Mountain Depression Glass Society; http://members.aol.com/iwantglass/indexg5.html. Information on meetings and shows.

RECOMMENDED READING

Collector's Encyclopedia of Fiesta: Plus Harlequin, Riviera, and Kitchen Kraft by Bob and Sharon Huxford (Collector Books, 2000).

Still sturdy and useful, Fiesta remains an affordable collection.

RECYCLING

■ SAVED FROM THE WRECKING BALL: ARCHITECTURAL ARTIFACTS

by NIKI HAYDEN

In the world of antiques, architectural artifacts are the leftovers—the doors, mantels, windows, and hardware. China, silver, glassware, furniture, and jewelry may be handed from grandparent to grandchild, but architectural remnants come only from one painful episode—demolition.

Architectural artifacts include stained glass windows from mansions and churches.

Monasteries, turn-of-the-century homes, grand ballrooms, hotels, civic gardens—urban renewal is worldwide, and the trash it creates becomes treasure somewhere else.

"When I got started in the mid-seventies," says Tom Sundheim, owner of Architectural Artifacts in Denver, "I was amazed at how many classical buildings were bulldozed over. I'd arrive with a pickup and pack of beer and would remove things from commercial buildings and mansions. Urban renewal was rampant. I had an appreciation for the artistic craftsmanship as it was discarded."

TURN-OF-THE-CENTURY AMERICANA MOST POPULAR

Tom's store is filled with turn-of-the-century finds—stained glass windows, shelves, urinals, bathtubs, cabinets, and doors. His large store has the ambience of an old warehouse, with labyrinthine paths that allow meandering from hardware to stained glass, brass to doors. In the first decade of business, inventory came strictly from Denver. As old neighborhoods were pulled down to make way for convention centers, Tom knew that glass doorknobs and brass hardware were too beautiful and too well made to be sent to a landfill. He could sell good-looking stuff on the side of the road.

Fence portions, hardware, bathtubs—all are potential for recycling.

Now, old mansions are less likely to be taken down. It's the strip malls that more commonly meet the wrecker's ball. Or, the historical buildings are taken down so quickly that Tom has no time to salvage any piece at all. "It's called crush and rush," he says.

Much of his inventory now comes from the Midwest, where his first love, turn-of-the-century Americana, reigns. The Midwest also is the primary plucking ground for Carrie and Tim Wise, who specialize in mantels and fireplaces. Their Niwot shop is nestled among the antique stores of the Old Town. At first glance, the shop looks like a fireplace factory, circa 1890. Mantels lean against the walls—all kinds and varieties—looking stranded and forlorn. Selling mantels is a rare specialty within a specialty. For the Wises, it came about by happenstance.

One of the most popular artifacts is an old-fashioned mantel.

Eight years ago, Tim was refinishing furniture when he received his first mantel. His location, plopped in the middle of thousands of new houses, proved serendipitous. Customers, he says, "liked the look. A mantel makes a house a little more than just a tract home with a tile fireplace."

Old tiles and hardware are culled from demolished homes.

And the proof is that buyers are taking the mantels with them when they move. It's no longer a part of the house, but private furniture. Tim often sells another mantel to the new buyers who purchase the house. Fortunately, the sizes of mantels—usually thirty-six or forty-two inches—haven't varied much in the last hundred years, and that makes selling them viable.

Tim specializes in the Victorian or turn-of-the-century period; the wood is usually golden oak. Everyday prices made oak a standard back then. Oak remains popular, he says, perhaps because the settling of Colorado began in earnest at the end of the nineteenth century, when Victorian oak was all the rage. Tim also carries a few mantels in mahogany, a pricier and imported wood of the same era.

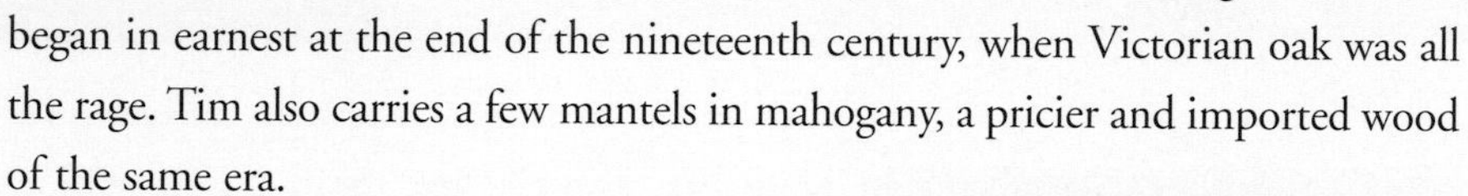

The difference between furniture and mantels is that mantels and fireplaces arrive with layers of paint. Each piece has to be stripped and restored. Once, it was simply a fixture of a house, but now it has become furniture.

Stained glass is always in demand.

Tom and Tim cater to the do-it-yourselfers: those who want to refurbish an old home, or add a touch of practical history to the new. But there's another category of architectural artifacts. In some cases artifacts simply have to stand on their own. They won't fit into modern or Victorian American architecture.

Garden statuary, iron fencing, and wooden benches are destined for new gardens.

Seeing Artifacts as Works of Art

"I see them as objects with texture and scale and design—art in their own right," Eron Johnson says. And, like Tom, he collected architectural pieces years before it became a popular pastime. "I always wanted to build a castle," he says, and simply began collecting pieces one by one—a door here, an archway there, a gate or a portion of a fence.

Eron's large store is filled with furniture, china—all the elements of a well-appointed antiques emporium. You'll have to find the narrow stairs to the floor below to see the architectural finds. There, where the light is low, you'll squeeze through the aisles to discover doors and windows, pillars and columns.

He travels to the likely spots—France, Italy, and Portugal—to find seventeenth-century monastic wooden doors. These won't fit any modern doorway. Instead, they lean against the wall like minimalist sculpture. He also scours India, where urban renewal has taken hold. There he uncovers doors made from precious woods, hand carved. Eron looks at them as art pried away from the original context.

Spain is another favorite destination. "I'm lucky to be in the part of the country that has a bit of Hispanic history. You don't see this in Tennessee," he says.

Although some of his customers come from outside Colorado, Denver is where Eron was born and raised—so he caters to Coloradans. Much of his aesthetic has been shaped by the Spanish influences throughout Colorado. Just as Mexico and Colorado once were farflung lands of the Spanish colonial empire, Eron sees value in artifacts from other colonial eras: "I've been buying colonial pieces in India. You'll get a French cabinet made from rosewood." Dutch and English influence a style, but a piece might be made out of satinwood—a wood not to be found in Holland or England.

Monastery doors and wooden statuary—whatever is thrown away by one culture may be prized by another.

In this country, he says, "there's a finite amount. I collected almost every category from silver to American folk art, metal working, sculpture, majolica—but this—the architectural—is my first love."

Passion for architectural artifacts is a sign that we may not be the throwaway culture we were twenty years ago. Now we savor even the hardware from the past. Yet, as Eron reminds us, prizing the materials of building may finally be gaining popularity and status, but like all antiques, they eventually become rare.

RESOURCES

DEALERS

Architectural Antiques, 2669 Larimer Street, Denver, 80205; 303-297-9722; www.archantiques.com.

Architectural Artifacts, 2207 Larimer Street, Denver, 80205; 303-292-6012; www.abqueencity.com.

Architectural Salvage, 5001 North Colorado Boulevard, Denver, 80216; 303-321-0200.

Architectural Stuff, 3970 South Broadway, Englewood, 80110; 303-761-2999.

Do-It-Ur-Self Plumbing & Heating Supply, 3120 Brighton Boulevard, Denver, 80216; 303-297-0455. Antique and reproduction bathroom and kitchen fixtures; reglazing and radiators.

Eron Johnson Antiques, Ltd., 451 Broadway, Denver, 80203; 303-777-8700; www.eronjohnsonantiques.com.

Paris Blue, 350 Kalamath Street, Denver, 80223; 720-932-6200. Variety of antiques with a French touch.

Raven Architectural Artifacts, 600 North Second Street, LaSalle, 80645; 970-284-0921.

Specialty Architectural Products, 2400 East Colfax Avenue, Denver, 80206; 303-316-9300.

Wise Buys Antiques, 190 Second Avenue, P.O. Box 153, Niwot, 80544; 303-652-2888.

■ Brush Up: Auctions and Painted Furniture

by LINDSEY LAFON

Down in the basement, tucked between the table saw and terra cotta planters, sits Uncle Bob's chair. It was added to my earthly possessions about a decade ago.

Sporting evidence of several colorful paint jobs, nicked and dinged, the chair has been a trustworthy, impromptu sawhorse, a stepstool, and more. It's sturdy, with its joinery intact—a humble and useful bit of my shop life.

Uncle Bob's chair is about to get a new look.

Home-Crafted or Commissioned

With a weekend's effort and a few dollars of materials, you can transform the forlorn to the reborn, worthy of star status placement in your favorite room. It's the perfect project for an artsy weekend, a four-legged canvas for your creativity. And in the hands of an artist, a mundane piece of furniture can be transformed into a signature, room-defining *objet.*

Debra Miner has been applying her talents to furniture, walls, and architectural details for over a decade. Using an array of faux finish painting techniques, she can turn a basic drywall surface into a textured wall of ochre that would do a Tuscan villa proud. A simple wooden column is magically transformed into carved granite, subtly speckled with bits of coral. An entryway comes alive with the soft effect of parchment washed in warm tones.

"A lot of houses are big and white and cold," Debra says. "We'll go in and paint a room in beige or taupe to give it warmth. I've done bedrooms and bathrooms in relaxing sage colors. And we've done dining rooms in deep reds, cabernet, and purple," adding a dramatic touch to dinners at home.

Practically all of these painting techniques work equally well when applied to furniture. A color-washed garden bench welcomes guests to the front door. Set among more traditional pieces, an armoire with hand-painted flowers creates a colorful focal point in the bedroom.

Debra's first foray into painted furniture was no small effort. "I opened a natural food restaurant in Middletown, New York, in 1986, and I painted all of the furniture—forty chairs and a dozen tables. I even 'marbleized' the refrigerators," she laughs.

Since then, she has focused her efforts on individual pieces. "I did a table with faux marble legs, and then added bottle caps, dice, and dominoes for a mosaic effect."

A nondescript white vinyl chair went exotic when she added black tiger stripes.

For daughter Isabelle's bedroom, Debra gave an armoire a base coat of green, covering it with hand-painted small roses and polka dots.

"It's girly whimsical, that's how I would describe it," she says.

The armoire stands amid walls of buttery yellow, and, divided by the stripe of a white chair rail, soothing sage. "I actually brought butter in and matched the color," she says. Debra then painted roses and vines to add to the fantasy room.

Ingenuity and paint transform old furniture of no particular value.

Artist Shari Rogoff uses the ancient art of trompe l'oeil to transform furniture and walls into illusions of wonder. The French term means to "deceive or trick the eye." This technique manipulates our depth perception to create the illusion that items represented in paint are actually real. Objects appear to protrude forward; backgrounds fall away convincingly.

It's an old craft, with historical references as early as Pliny the Elder in fifth-century Athens. Rembrandt's students reportedly painted coins on the floor of his studio for the puckish pleasure of watching him try to retrieve them.

Shari, who has a degree in fine arts with an emphasis in oil painting, did her first furniture piece in New York City in 1989. "Southwestern was hot then," she recalls. "I painted a large buffet with doors and cabinets in turquoise and greens. It took about two weeks to do."

Working steadily for six years with architects and designers, Shari helped create sample kitchens for an English custom woodworker. She also painted a floor to resemble a fine Oriental rug."I did a lot of kids' stuff, too. It's not as serious. It fits the style; it's fun."

Shari, who creates her trompe l'oeil pieces on a commission basis, says that a typical large piece can take up to fifteen hours to finish. "And that's for a piece that is not real complicated, but does have some detail. Distressed pieces don't take as long—mostly you are just waiting for it to dry in between coats of paint or stain." A smaller piece, such as a chair, might take four hours start to finish.

Isabelle's room combines freshly painted furniture and painted walls.

The most popular treatment right now is the distressed, rustic look, Shari says. Furniture is made to look old; layers of paint expose tantalizing scratches of vibrant color, revealed from underneath.

Depending on your taste, Shari can create in paint whatever you wish to imagine. But the "keeper" pieces—the ones that are timeless but not trendy—draw from simple, classic traditions, such as country French or Tuscany—even colonial.

"Think about what your parents liked," suggests Shari. "It's the stuff they liked enough to keep. I have a great swing on my porch—I know this sounds like Martha Stewart—it's painted robin's egg blue, and I love it."

Both Debra and Shari charge approximately $800 to $900 for a piece such as an armoire or large chest. A smaller piece, such as a chair, would run around $200. As is true with all commissioned art, each piece is unique, and so is the deal you make with your artist.

Do-It-Yourself

And now, we're ready for some hands-on time with Uncle Bob's chair. As I mentioned earlier, this can be a fun and creative project to work on over a weekend.

I've got my brushes and sponges, latex primer, and several cans of paint. I have collected rags, newspapers, and drop cloths. Cold beverages are as near as the fridge.

I will be working in the garage, with lots of room and an open door for ventilation.

After drop cloths are diligently arranged (hey, we're painting furniture here—something's bound to get spilled!), set the piece in the middle of your work area. If it is a smaller piece, consider devising some kind of workbench or table to set your project on. It will save your lower back some anguish, I promise.

Both Debra and Shari recommend using only water-based acrylic or latex paints. They are less toxic, easier to clean, and take much less time to dry. If you will be painting over an oil-based finish (quite likely, if you are working on an older piece of furniture) you will want to sand the piece, then apply a latex primer coat. Let the primer coat dry, and then lightly sand once again.

As for tools, again both of our experts agree: used or inexpensive brushes are best. If you are going for an antique or distressed look, you will need to get aggressive with your tools, so you don't want to use a brand-new, top-of-the-line brush. "You pretty much ruin a brush when you do a color wash," says Debra. "I use cheap ones, called 'chip' brushes."

Shari uses razor blades, chains, and a hammer to add rustic "character" to her pieces, if needed.

For layers of texture, you can apply the paint with sponges or rags. Work lightly, and don't get too much paint on your sponge, or you will lose the effect. Debra says that she doesn't use sponges much anymore, preferring the softer, subtler effect of color washing. Allow plenty of drying time between coats of paint. Latex dries fast, so a couple hours is usually sufficient.

When you are finished applying paint, you will want to protect your masterpiece with a final latex urethane coat. A simple clean up with a damp sponge is all the maintenance needed with a finished piece.

Uncle Bob's chair now sports two shades of ochre, with highlights of metallic gold peeking through.

As soon as I get that final urethane coat on, we'll be sitting pretty.

The Auction: "Five...Give Me Ten"

If you don't have an orphaned piece of furniture sitting around, you can usually find some pretty good deals at used furniture stores. Flea markets and garage sales are great sources, too.

Or you could visit your nearest unfinished furniture outlet. You will find all types of tables, chests, and chairs ready for their brush with fame. A basic chair can be found for as little as $40, and a child's rush-seated rocker runs around $50. Smaller side tables or plant stands are in the same price bracket. You don't have to spend a lot to try your hand at furniture painting.

But to have the most fun while searching for that project piece, check out one of the area's antiques and furniture auctions, usually held on Sundays. Scan the weekend classifieds for auction notices, or visit auction websites.

Two auctions worth the visit are the Rawhide Auction in Berthoud and the Niwot Auction at the Boulder County Fairgrounds in Longmont. Visit the websites (see the Resources section at the end of this chapter) for auction dates and directions.

Auctions are a good place to locate used furniture.

You'll see a vast assortment of items, mostly mundane but sometimes magnificent. Weirdly styled kitchen contraptions, medieval-looking lawn implements, and ceramic lamps with dubious provenance all take their turns on the auction block. And then, there is the furniture.

Each auction offers its own unique collections and specialties, but typically you will find at least a dozen large pieces, such as buffets, chests of drawers, and tables. Scattered among them are various chairs: bentwood café chairs (a set of five, alas, not six), a mission oak rocker, and less distinguished constructions.

We are looking for something on the humble side, as befits our do-it-yourself expertise, so we won't be bruising the bank account much.

Be sure to arrive early enough to check out what's available. To allow potential bidders to peruse, most auctions open their doors two hours before things get under way. Look for furniture that has not been abused. Banged up and scratched will work, but you want to avoid big, visible gouges. And stay away from anything with significant water damage. You want to paint furniture, not restore its soul.

Check the joinery. If it's a chair, do the rungs still support the legs? Will a simple re-gluing get it back on its feet? Pull each individual drawer out from chests, checking how smoothly it travels. How are the bottoms of the drawers? Any significant warping can make it difficult to open and shut drawers.

Walk around the piece if possible, so you see it from every angle. If it looks promising, write down on your notepad (you brought a notepad, right?) the number of the piece. Decide the most that you are willing to pay, and write that number down, too.

If you are going to bid on anything, you will need to register with the auctioneer. After providing the basic personal information and specifying your means of payment (larger auctions accept Visa and MasterCard, and you can often get up to a 2 percent discount by paying cash), you will be issued a card with a large number on it.

Once the bargaining begins, pay attention to closing prices on similar pieces of furniture. This will help you bid reasonably when your piece is on the block.

The auctioneer's patter may seem downright undecipherable at first. It's fast paced, designed to keep things moving. Listen for the two numbers that he is repeating. The lower number is the current bid, and the higher number is the bid to raise. If things are moving slowly, the auctioneer will lower the raise amount, honing in on the final offer.

Look for wooden details that can be defined with paint.

To bid on an item, just raise your card so the auctioneer can see it. Your bid will be acknowledged by number. Keep in mind your top price and stick to it. You want to go home happy. Did you make the winning bid? Go over to the payment window and take care of business, then go to the claims area and collect your prize.

Load up the van, make a stop at the paint store, and let the fun begin!

RESOURCES

■ AUCTIONS

Ferrell Auction Company, 5505 West Highway 34, Loveland, 80537; 970-635-0044; www.ferrellauction.com.

Niwot Auction, Boulder County Fairgrounds, 9595 Nelson Road, Longmont, 80501; 303-776-6490; www.niwotauction.com.

Rawhide Auction, 349 Massachusetts Avenue, Berthoud, 80513; 970-532-3034; www.rawhideauction.com.

■ DO-IT-YOURSELF WEBSITES

Do It Yourself Furniture Refinishing; www.refinishfurniture.com.

Do It Yourself Network; www.diynet.com.

Guiry's Color Source; www.guirys.com. Guiry's offers paints, wallpaper, and art supplies. One of the largest suppliers in Colorado. Six locations:

Denver (LoDo): 2245 Market Street; 303-292-0444

Denver (University Hills): 2468 D. Colorado Boulevard; 303-758-8244

Littleton: 8170 South University Boulevard; 303-770-2572

Littleton (Southwest Plaza): 9046 West Bowles Avenue; 303-972-9393

Arvada: 8700 Wadsworth Boulevard; 303-456-8030

Boulder: 2870 28th Street; 303-444-3800

ANTIQUE HUNTING: ONE OF SUMMER'S PLEASURES

by CAROL WARD

Up, up, I force myself out of bed on a Saturday summer morning, knowing that I have no time for makeup or any fashion sense. I am an "antiquer" and summer weekend mornings are prime time.

I'm delighted when I see people spring cleaning. The need to clean out one's house might be primal, but what I want to know is—what are you getting rid of that I might want? I'm off to my neighborhood and territory beyond.

With the many yard sales, open-air flea markets, house sales, and auctions, shopping takes on new proportions. It's all about options and knowing that any road can lead to a treasure.

Most endeavors can be better accomplished if you have a plan. This is true of treasure hunting. I've already circled the classified sections of my Thursday and Friday newspapers, and I've mapped out my route. So with map, pen, and paper in hand, I jump in my car.

Through bleary eyes I see that I've scratched off the first address. Children's toys and clothing, always a popular draw, don't interest me. I head straight to my next address that has listed "pottery, household items, and much more." A dry run to that address the day before puts me right in front of the house a few minutes before 8:00 A.M.—the start time listed in the paper.

I consider myself lucky when I find a small yellow McCoy flowerpot for $20 and an old wire egg basket for only $.50. McCoy pieces in good condition are highly sought after these days and I've noticed these particular egg baskets in antique shops for $20 to $40.

Most sales start early. I've seen a few ads state that "early birds will be flogged," but by and large, doors and gates open earlier. Try to contain your enthusiasm if you arrive too early. The inhabitants will probably still be sleeping. If they don't open their doors on time, you can get rowdy.

College students moving out of their apartments for the summer may not have what you want. But a word of advice here: If you have time, take a look. You never know what you will find. Then you can quickly size up the sale and move on if it's not for you.

Quilts are held up for viewing at an auction.

I recently found a wonderful old wicker breakfast bed tray at a small yard sale run by two twenty-somethings in Boulder. The wicker was at least twice their combined ages. Dusty with cobwebs, it was in excellent condition and I gladly paid their asking price of $20.

Prices are usually low and reasonable at yard sales. There's not too much room to bargain, but if you think there is, go ahead and ask for a better price. An acquaintance of mine bought two authentic pieces of Navajo jewelry for under $15 at a local yard sale in Longmont. He also found two sterling silver Scandinavian bracelets at $10! They were in excellent condition and *old*. I know because I bought one from him—an exquisitely sculptured antique sterling cuff bracelet. I paid a considerably higher price. How did I miss that yard sale?

Bargains and Caveats for Flea Markets

Another great buying venue is the flea market. Originating from the French phrase *marché aux puces,* it means "a specially designated occasion for the purpose of exchanging a wide variety of goods." And in those days, there were fleas flying around the old and odd pieces of furniture in the European markets.

In today's typical flea market, you'll find fewer fleas and many items—from antiques and collectibles to new close-out items and everything in between.

It helps to know what you are looking for. Ask questions, and distinguish between the valuable and, well, junk.

The Front Range offers its fair share of flea markets. But they're not an antiquer's paradise. What you will find is a sea of socks, sneakers, car tires, used and new children's clothing, toys, and much, much more.

You can find flea markets throughout the country and the world. One of the most popular is the Rose Bowl flea market in Pasadena, California. It ranks as the largest and best known in the country and has operated on the grounds of the Rose Bowl for the past thirty-two years. You can do some celebrity watching, too, when you take a break from your bargain hunting. Diane Keaton, among other Hollywood celebs, has been seen picking through the goods. It's held the second Sunday of each month, rain or shine.

Small items are auctioned first while a sea of furniture waits behind.

Don't forget to visit flea markets when you are traveling abroad. Find out in advance or ask when you get in where the flea markets are. This is a must in certain cities, such as Paris and London.

In Paris go to the Marché aux Puces. Started over a century ago, this market put itself on the map when masterpiece paintings were found by chance in the 1920s. It runs Saturday through Monday, year-round.

The Marché aux Puces is located outside the Porte de Clignancourt Metro station (Line 4-Porte d'Orleans to Porte de Clignancourt). It is just due north at the edge of Paris.

I was in Budapest recently, looking forward to the flea market I'd read about in the travel guide. What the travel guide didn't say was that the market was only held on Saturdays, which is typical of a number of European cities. Having arrived on Sunday to leave on Friday, I missed it. I was directed to another flea market, but it was in a town that was too far and inconvenient for me to make the trip.

If you're a serious antique shopper, I suggest London's Bermondsey Market, also called the New Caledonia Market. It's open all day on Sundays, but go very early for the best deals. Just walk over the Tower Bridge (south) to the crossroad, past a vinegar factory, turn right, and you are there. There are others, such as the currently trendy Camden Lock Market in Camden Town for clothing, jewelry, and antiques, or the ever-popular Portobello Road Market in the West End.

Auctions: Something Completely Different

If you can stand a little excitement, auctions are a wonderful way to find different and interesting pieces. You will pay one-half of retail prices and sometimes even less. There is an excitement and element of surprise when you bid at auction. You never know what you are going to go home with, which could be a good *or* a bad thing.

Always go early to the preview. Check the items you plan to bid on very thoroughly. Write down or have in your mind the ceiling price—the highest price that you are willing to go. Once the bidding gets going, it can be mind numbing. And when the hammer comes down on your winning bid, it's yours. There is no return receipt.

Auctions are a year-round event. But, as antiques dealer Richard Miller says, "If you want to sell a piece, sell in the winter, if you want to buy, buy in the summer." Due to the many alternatives in the summer months, fewer people attend auctions. We're all just too busy in the summer running from yard sale to flea market to house sale.

Don't Overlook House and Estate Sales

House sales may be the best-kept secret of all buying options. While auction prices climb higher and flea markets bulge with new and low-end items, house sales hold promise.

Last Saturday I "hit" three house sales. At the first one, I bought six pieces of Frankoma pottery, a set that included two cups and saucers, a creamer, and a sugar bowl with lid for a total of $8. I thought it was an early pattern, but when I turned the pieces over, the clay was a reddish-brown indicating that these particular pieces were made after 1956 when the Frankoma Pottery Company moved to Sapulpa, Oklahoma.

Earlier wares were made from a light cream-colored—almost beige—clay, when they were located in Ada, Oklahoma. But that was okay, because aside from the low price, they were well-made pieces in perfect condition. Quality items will increase in value over time.

On a shady tree-lined street in a suburb of Denver, I located my second house. Arriving just twenty minutes after the posted time, I was very surprised to see several pieces of furniture already loaded on a truck, rooms cleared out, and people paying for their newly acquired items.

I inquired and was told that when the sellers saw the crowd, they let them in an hour earlier! See what I mean? Wonderful items were "walking" out the door right past me. I would have loved the two lamps that screamed art deco, but their new owner was already protectively hugging them to her chest.

In my crushed but hopeful spirit, I spied a stack of white and red dinner plates on the kitchen counter. Turning them over I saw they were Buffalo China. Strong and sturdy china made in Buffalo, New York, in the early 1900s, these plates were destined for restaurants as was the Syracuse and some of the Fire King China. If you see any of this china—buy it! The prices are skyrocketing. I counted eleven plates, all in good condition.

"What do you want for them?" I asked a fellow who looked like he lived there. His response surprised and thrilled me. "Four dollars," he said. Fortunately for me, he was not a man who knew his china. I whipped out a five and didn't bother to wait for the change. On my way out, I paused to watch a fellow in the corner mulling over three fabulous oil paintings. My growing impatience to interrupt and make an offer was extinguished when I heard him say he'd take them all.

The last house was a disappointment. It looked as though the house sale had taken place the day before. It was practically empty. I took a fast look around. I managed to snag a book on the Civil War and a 1946 edition of Dante Alighieri's *The Divine Comedy,* which was in good condition and had a lovely decorative hardcover. Books abound at house sales. On my way out I paid $.50 for the two books and threw in a dollar for a tall amaryllis plant sitting by the door looking longingly for a new home.

Prior to the auction, potential buyers mill around, searching for that one-of-a-kind item they've been looking for.

The sun was beating down and it wasn't even noon yet. I headed home with all my purchases tucked in the back seat and trunk of my car. I can't say I found a treasure, but I found some good usable items at low prices. And while you're looking around, don't forget to look for treasures in your own backyard, attic, and basement—and you don't have to wait until spring.

Tips for Successful Treasure Hunting

- Always start out early.
- Know or learn the lay of the land by making advance dry runs. Have a map and a plan, otherwise you'll waste valuable time.
- Dress for the weather and weather changes. In the Front Range that means hats, sun protection, and sunglasses.

- Wear comfortable shoes and clothing.
- Bring food if you don't want to take precious time away from your shopping.
- Bring cash with lots of lower denomination bills.
- Bring along some of your own bags and boxes for your purchases.
- Don't bring along chatty friends who will slow you down.
- Always ask for a better price, but do it in a nice way.
- Bring along a current price guide, but remember that prices listed are usually conservative.
- Take a look most anywhere and remember to look above and below table level.

RESOURCES

MAJOR FRONT RANGE FLEA MARKETS

COLORADO SPRINGS

The Flea Market, 5225 East Platte Avenue, Colorado Springs, 80915; 719-380-8599.
Open 7 A.M. to 4 P.M., Saturday and Sunday.

DENVER AREA

Mile High Flea Market, 7007 East 88th Avenue, Henderson, 80640; 303-289-4656.
Open 7 A.M. to 5 P.M., Wednesday, Saturday, and Sunday.

Ballpark Flea Market, outdoors at 22nd and Larimer Streets, Denver; www.ballparkmarket.com.
Seasonal, so check the website for schedules.

FORT COLLINS

Foothills Flea Market and Fort Collins Flea Market, daily, 10 A.M. to 6 P.M. Location: 6200 and 6300 South College, just off I-25, between Fort Collins and Loveland on Highway 287, 80525; 970-223-9069.

LOVELAND

The Great Colorado Marketplace, 6701 Marketplace Drive, I-25 at exit 254, Loveland, 80537; 970-278-1900.

Not So Old, but Loved

Nifty Fifties: Arapahoe Acres Celebrates Modernism in Colorado

by NIKI HAYDEN

Glance at the National Register of Historic Places, which notes remarkable buildings and neighborhoods in America, and you'll find plenty of colonial town squares and elegant Victorian streets. We're accustomed to anything over one hundred years old becoming a revered site. So it's all the more jolting to realize a neighborhood just south of Denver, in Englewood, is also listed on the register. It dates to the 1950s, the first neighborhood in the United States to be listed from that era.

The houses in Arapahoe Acres showcase modernism after World War II.

Arapahoe Acres includes 124 houses built from 1949 to 1957. A brainchild of Colorado builder Edward Hawkins and Czech-born architect Eugene Sternberg, the pattern of homes marries European modernism and Frank Lloyd Wright's Usonian style with bold and brash flourishes. The neighborhood is like a laboratory, showcasing exciting new architectural ideas of the time. A post–World War II optimism encouraged breaking away from vertical and ornamented buildings and experimenting with the most basic of forms—whether horizontal or cubed.

Today, a few of the original homeowners still live in the neighborhood, but most houses are occupied by a new generation that treasures the styles and influences of the 1950s, with its strong geometric lines, unusual rooflines, open construction, and vibrant use of stone, glass, and brick.

Modernism takes a cubist approach.

Stop by the home of Yvonne and Dave Steers and you're likely to hear the strains of Frank Sinatra. "We lived in a bungalow in Washington Park," Yvonne says, "but we've sold our antiques. And now we're collecting some furniture from the fifties that will fit in." They believe the neighborhood to be unique—a collection of homes where any passerby can tour their streets and be cast back to a narrow window of time when American architecture changed forever.

Reclaiming the Recent Past

Yvonne and Dave toured southern California after they moved into their new home, making a pilgrimage to the house of the dynamic duo of fifties design, Charles and Ray Eames. Originators of the famed Eames chair and a host of recognizable fifties forms, the Eameses' Los Angeles home is not open to the public, but enthusiasts like Yvonne and Dave are allowed to walk around the premises. "It hardly mattered," Yvonne says. "The house is glass and you can see into it." With architectural thoughts swirling in their heads, they returned, ready to reclaim the recent past.

Yvonne and Dave Steers traded in a bungalow for a house that takes them back to the 1950s.

Their long, horizontal home is studded with red bricks, broken to expose a textured edge. Trapezoidal

Natural stone and local brick were regional products refashioned for a sleek new look.

windows line up below the ceiling, which is made from tongue-in-groove pine planks. Dave researched the original look of his home and then set off for salvage yards, lighting stores, and manufacturers that have continued lines of linoleum or cork flooring suitable for the 1950s.

"Several of us sat down with the original general contractor, Clyde Mannon, who is still alive and in Golden, today," he says. "There was mahogany used all around the house, including doors, paneling, cabinets. He told me it was almost as cheap as pine then, so they used it all over."

Dave returned to mahogany for a slanted sink vanity and built-in wall cabinet in a bathroom. Large six-by-six-inch green tiles line up, accented with thin black tiles. The opening to the shower is narrow—more so than you'd find today. And the bathroom mirror and lights, sturdy and utilitarian, hold their own in solid materials meant to last forever.

Like the exterior, the interior starkly states the obvious: strong, useful, brash, and simple, with nothing flimsy. Only the basic building materials are allowed to be ornamental. And little is built without attention to its purpose. In a master bedroom, a partition wall hints at Japanese influence, as if it's a screen, almost floating, but affixed by a single post with mahogany trim. The

Mahogany cabinets, stainless steel sinks, and vintage tiles are part of the Steers's home.

connection is elegant but serves a crucial purpose. "It's not covered with Sheetrock as most new homes are," Dave explains, as he points to overhead beams.

Modernism—A Social Ideal

The architecture in Arapahoe Acres echoes social ideas as profound as the buildings. Sternberg embraced a philosophy that architecture mattered to the ordinary person, and so set about to create modest homes with striking lines. European immigrant architects arrived in America with functional Bauhaus design principles, new egalitarian ideals, and attention to engineering. Sternberg was no exception.

Bringing together the outdoors and indoors remains an element of design in the neighborhood.

Hawkins had soaked up the ideas of Frank Lloyd Wright during a stay in Chicago. When Wright turned to populist architecture during the Great Depression, builders like Hawkins took notice. Together, Hawkins and Sternberg, caught up in the excitement of modern architecture's international style, started with affordable homes that would catch the attention of major home and architecture magazines. They also paid homage to the aging Wright.

In a photo dated 1948, Wright visits the University of Denver, where Sternberg taught. A young architect, Gerry Dion, who, much later, would design homes for Arapahoe Acres, stands next to him. Wright is unmistakable. Elegantly attired, he holds a soft fedora hat in hand. At a time when the men surrounding him sport short haircuts, Wright's gray hair hangs over his ears, like the silky ears of a spaniel. He's the center of attention, the young architects smiling with reverence and awe. Although Wright designed but never built in Colorado, his ideas are evident throughout Arapahoe Acres.

You'll see his influence in the prevalence of natural materials: large glass panels that marry the outdoors and indoors. Cork, wood, and brick are design principles as well as building blocks. Many of the homes are long and horizontal, mirroring the Japanese and prairie influences that seeped into Wright's architecture. Homes are nestled into gentle slopes, like cherries dropped into a puff of whipped cream. Their horizontal lines hug the landscape.

An unusual butterfly roof is one architectural break from the past.

But Wright is not the only influence. You'll see the international style, too. Some homes are shaped as cubes with windows as the major accent. Garage doors hang flush with the walls, all the more to unify the unaccented exterior. Roofs are flat or butterfly-shaped.

Neighbors Research Their History

The neighborhood was intriguing enough to interest architecture consultant Diane Wray. Early modernism, caught in the swing of the wrecker's ball, was disappearing. Soon, she noticed, we would be saving the early decade of the twentieth century and living in the early decade of the twenty-first century. In between, all would be lost. When Diane returned to Denver from New York, she looked up former classmates—all architecture enthusiasts. "We were interested in buildings we loved in Denver and formed the Modern Architecture Preservation League," she says.

Friends urged her to visit Arapahoe Acres, where she settled into a small early house designed by Hawkins: "One of my neighbors said living here was 'just like Brigadoon.' Although you see other houses of this period, there's nothing that competes with Arapahoe Acres in terms of the integrity of site design, houses, and street design."

Carports and wide streets signaled the new importance of the automobile in the 1950s.

Wray and several neighbors began collecting the history, interviewing surviving architects and builders. They submitted their historic district nomination to the Colorado Historical Society, which eventually endorsed and passed it on to the National Park Service, the oversight organization for the National Register.

Still, choosing Arapahoe Acres was always a choice from the heart. It wasn't an easy project for Hawkins to build in the 1950s, when federal guidelines for government housing loans insisted on traditional housing. It's not easy today to preserve modest homes when the trend is toward massive square footage.

"Instead of adding on," Diane says about her 858-square-foot home, "my goal is to pare down my life to fit into the house. If you look at the Usonian design, it was not just about a house, but a way of life. It represents a whole collision of social, architectural, and technological issues that came about as a result of World War II. The amount of privacy afforded is astounding. Although this is a tiny house, the layout of rooms seems spacious. No more servants; no elaborate meals. Yet,

Horizontal lines, wide expanses of glass and brick—all were design elements in Arapahoe Acres.

every house has a fireplace no matter how small. And, the automobile was playing into this."

It's impossible not to notice the influence of the automobile on Arapahoe Acres. Wide, curving streets signal the importance of a car. Carports change to garages, which expand and take on prominence in the later, larger homes. The earliest homes, modest and practical, give way, in time, to more expensive houses. Sternberg and Hawkins parted ways on this issue but remained friends.

The last homes, which take on a more dramatic scale in the size of windows, reveal the rise in prosperity within a decade. Early homes may have represented a triumph for the working American over the Great Depression, but later homes indicate the glimmerings of sustained good times.

Back in the Steerses' kitchen, Dave pulls out a collection of photos. The original owners moved years ago to a larger home in Arapahoe Acres, but the two families are friends. A small photo catches a woman at the counter: pointy glasses, bouffant hair, full skirt, and tidy apron.

Outside her home, a popular general, Dwight D. Eisenhower, steers the nation through a world in turmoil. A young man named Fidel Castro foments a revolution in Cuba. Troubling McCarthy hearings air on television. The Soviet Union's leader, Nikita Khrushchev, proves to be a wild card.

Strong geometric shapes define each home.

But at her stove, spatula in hand, dinner is nearly ready in the long galley kitchen. The soft tones of Nat King Cole float high and clear. Light filters through high windows and fills the interior. And although there's no basement or attic, no stairs, no traditional floor plan or conventional use of space, the woman is smiling—she's at the epicenter of the new modern look and her home has plenty of style.

RESOURCES

■ HISTORIC DISTRICT

Arapahoe Acres, c/o Dave Steers 3058 South Cornell Circle, Englewood, 80110; www.arapahoeacres.org.

■ ACCURATE REPLACEMENT PARTS

A & A Tradin Post (an Ace Hardware), 4509 South Broadway, Englewood, 80110; 303-761-0747.

■ CONTEMPORARY INTERPRETATIONS

The Lighting Studio, 1024 Cherokee Street, Denver, 80204; 303-595-0900. Lighting fixtures, lamps, etc.

Room & Board, 222 Detroit Street, Denver, 80206; 303-332-6462; www.roomandboard.com. Modern furniture, including new reproduction and Eames furniture.

■ MUSEUMS

The Denver Art Museum, 100 West 14th Avenue Parkway, Denver, 80204; 720-865-5000; www.denverartmuseum.org. Has an excellent design wing devoted to early modern and contemporary design.

Vance Kirkland Museum and Foundation, 1311 Pearl Street, Denver, 80203; 303-832-8576; www.vancekirkland.org. Home to a notable collection.

■ HELPFUL ORGANIZATIONS

ORIGINAL FURNITURE, FURNISHINGS, AND OTHER DECORATIVE ITEMS

Crown Mercantile, 46 Broadway, Denver, 80203; 303-715-9693; www.crownmercantile.com. Besides original furniture, offers some reproductions and interpretations of decorative items.

Decade, 56 South Broadway, Denver, 80209; 303-733-2288. Offers some reproductions and interpretations of decorative items and clothing.

Modern Classics, 1388 South Broadway, Denver, 80210; 303-744-8999. Offers reproductions of original furniture designs.

Mod Livin', 5327 East Colfax Avenue, Denver, 80220; 720-941-9292. Huge selection of original mid-century furniture, furnishings, decorative items, clothing.

One Home, 1036 Speer Boulevard, Denver, 80204; 720-946-1505. Also offers design services.

Popular Culture, 1150 South Broadway, Denver, 80210; 303-777-1163.

Retro Rose, 7564 Grant Place, Arvada, 80002; 303-940-0326

Wazee Deco, 383 Corona Street, Denver, 80218; 303-293-2144; www.wazeedeco.com.

■ SALVAGE SUPPLIERS

Do-It-Ur-Self Plumbing & Heating Supply, 3120 Brighton Boulevard, Denver, 80216; 303-297-0455.

Garrett Lumber & Wrecking Co., 7360 Grape Street, Commerce City, 80022; 303-288-4946 (office), 303-288-5932 (yard).

■ Collecting American Folk Art: Ordinary Whimsy

by NIKI HAYDEN

Nan and David Pirnack began collecting American folk art forty-seven years ago, although they weren't aware of it at the time. It all started when they bought a house. Included in the purchase was a collection. Suddenly their trendy early-marriage Danish modern furniture looked drab, settled next to a nineteenth-century carousel horse. The Danish has disappeared. The horse, frozen in its gallop, remains.

Since then, they've seen the rise in collecting all antiques and count themselves among the members of a small but fanatical faction to be found among collectors of American folk art. "There have always been covens of folk art collectors that go way back," Nan says.

A carousel horse is one of Nan and David Pirnack's treasures.

Those covens of devotees are the collectors of New England weather vanes or embroidered samplers. Shaker furniture. Amish quilts. The Pirnacks also have collected weather vanes and quilts throughout the years. But they say that they are on the lookout for the unusual, the eccentric. They prefer the weather vane with a chimney sweep atop, or a crazy quilt depicting hands festooned with embroidered wedding rings. Nan loves old rag dolls with hand-carved heads. David also likes carved wooden pieces, anything that shows the hand of the maker.

Sometimes commercial signs make their way into folk art.

Folk Art Is Highly Personal and Handmade

The folk art that the Pirnacks collect and sell is not what would furnish a house. "It's handmade, one of a kind, and hard to find," Nan says. A nineteenth-century carved wooden barber's pole. A fierce eagle emerging from a felt background. A tin house with old-fashioned Christmas bulbs. Pie chests with punched stars. "It took me a while to realize that I had collected pieces that had stars somewhere on them," Nan says, as if she has unwittingly collected a talisman for good luck.

American folk art is highly personal. These pieces are from unknown artists constrained by making a living. Many were craftspeople highly skilled in woodworking or needle craft. Each longed to express a personal flight of fancy, an interpretation of beauty, or to personalize a gift. "I remember a beautiful clock shelf built into a house," David says. "The craftsman built it at night and worked on the house by day. It was a gift to the owner, who had allowed him to live in the house."

The anonymity makes the work humble, and usually overlooked. It may have been practical, like a quilt. But it didn't have to be. There are checkerboards handsomely painted, each as vivid and geometric as Amish quilts. Weather vanes

The American eagle poses in a tapestry.

only need to indicate the direction of the wind. The Pirnacks found one that also summons a chimney sweep. Like much of American folk art, it's a clever design within the perimeters of practicality.

By definition, American folk art is handmade. Like all definitions, collectors will stretch that a bit. The Pirnacks point to a machine-made image of Colonel Sanders, his original recipe for signage in Kentucky. And American folk art, in general terms, predates 1940, David says. But on the patio, Elvis stands, carved and clustered with rhinestones.

Outsider Art—A Recent Arrival

Elvis is from the tradition of outsider art. "Outsider art is new. It's practiced by the untrained, and often the artists are African American and from the South. It began in the Southeast and was shown in Atlanta. Many of the artists have become well known. In the last twenty years it has become recognized as a legitimate art form," Nan says.

Stars punched into metal decorate an old pie chest

"The medium is often quirky," David adds, "and in the last ten years, I've seen a lot of religious symbolism. There's even a museum now in Baltimore that specializes in outsider art."

In forty-seven years, their tastes have evolved. They're no longer devoted strictly to Americana. The popularity of American folk art means that prices have skyrocketed for good pieces. So the Pirnacks often look afar. They have found rustic pieces in France and Canada. But in most cases, the intentions of the maker are the same: useful objects are transformed into one-of-a-kind works.

The Future of Collecting

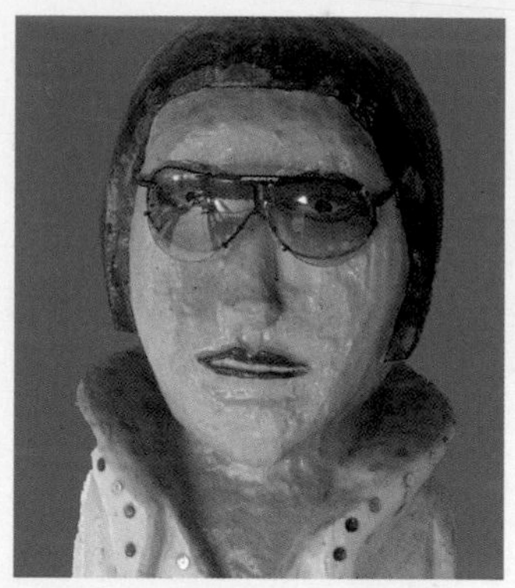

Elvis makes his presence these days in outsider art.

Americana antiques that once were affordable are available mostly to the well heeled these days. That usually omits collectors in the twenties and thirties age group. The Pirnacks see buyers who may be from forty to sixty, and it concerns them about the future of collecting. "Where are the younger dealers today?" Nan asks. Perhaps, they note, the platform for buying and selling antiques has shifted in a fundamental way.

"We've seen the collectors' market change in our lifetimes," David says and adds that he and Nan evolved from a storefront to malls and major antique shows. Now they are drifting toward sites like eBay. The auction sites on the Internet have transformed antique buying and selling like never before. Individual stores collect from locals; big shows pull in regional or national buyers. But the Internet has attracted a global audience. It's a boon to local dealers who simply have to wrap and ship their wares.

A weather vane also summons a chimney sweep.

"It can be cheap or wonderful," Nan says about what you might discover on auction websites. "They do give you a sense of value with the bids. They are changing the collectors' market." But change as it may, the whimsy so evident and wonderful in Americana folk art is inviting and endearing. Marketplaces may shift, but Elvis and Colonel Sanders, as we all know, endure.

APPENDIX

AMERICAN EARLY TWENTIETH CENTURY

Anything Antique or Unique, 124 South Union, Pueblo, 81003; 719-546-2596.

A Quartermoon Market, 315 East Pikes Peak, Colorado Springs, 80903; 719-633-3999.

Antique Legacy, 2624 West Colorado Avenue, Colorado Springs, 80904; 719-578-0637.

Antiques at Lincoln Park, 822 Eighth Street, Greeley, 80631; 970-351-6222.

Bennett Antiques, 1220 South College, Fort Collins, 80524; 970-482-3645; www.bennettantiques.com.

Brass Armadillo, Antique Mall, 11301 West I-70 Frontage Road, Wheat Ridge, 80033; 303-403-1677.

The Collection, 899 Broadway, Denver, 80203; 303-623-4200; www.antiquedesign.com.

Colorado Antique Gallery, 5501 South Broadway, Littleton, 80121; 303-794-8100.

Days Gone By Antiques, 356 Main Street, Longmont, 80501; 303-651-1912.

Karen's Antiques, 1415 South Broadway, Denver, 80210; 303-871-9922.

Main Street Antique Mall, 370 Main Street, Longmont, 80501; 303-776-8511.

Mezzanine Arts & Antiques, 127 West Main Street, Florence, 81226; 719-784-4598. Collection of vendors.

Niwot Antiques, 136 Second Avenue, Niwot, 80544; 303-652-2587.

Off Her Rocker Antiques, 4 East First Street, Nederland, 80466; 303-258-7976.

Old Century Antiques, 1202 West Colorado Avenue, Colorado Springs, 80904; 719-633-3439.

Page Antiques, 115 South Union Avenue, Pueblo, 81003; 719-543-2299.

Posh, 120 South Union Avenue, Pueblo, 81003; 719-253-2000.

Ralston Brothers Antiques, 425 High Street, Lyons, 80540; 303-823-6982.

Somewhere In Time, 220 South Union Avenue, Pueblo, 81003; 719-562-0885.

Twiggs, 165 Second Avenue, Niwot, 80544; 303-652-9065.

ANTIQUE DISTRICT

Denver Antique Row, 400–1800 South Broadway (and 25–27 East Dakota Avenue), Denver, 80210; 303-733-5251; www.antiques-colorado.com/antiquerow.

■ ANTIQUE SHOWS

Denver Antiques Show & Sale, to benefit the Central City Opera, 621 17th Street, Suite 1601, Denver, 80293; 303-292-6700; http://new.centralcityopera.org.

Denver Collectors' Fair, National Western Complex, I-70 at Brighton Boulevard, Denver; 303-526-7339. Held monthly.

Historic Boulder Street Market, 646 Pearl Street, Boulder, 80302; 303-444-5192; www.historicboulder.org. Saturdays, once a month, April–September.

Pumpkin Pie (autumn) and Strawberry Days Festivals (spring), Boulder County Fairgrounds, 9595 Hover Road, Longmont, 80501; 303-776-1870; www.st.vrainhistoricalsociety.org/antique.htm. Sponsored by the St. Vrain Historic Society.

World Wide Antique Shows, Denver Merchandise Mart, 451 East Fifty-eighth Avenue, Denver, 80216; 303-368-0040; www.wwantiqueshows.com.

■ APPRAISALS

Longmont Museum and Cultural Center, 400 Quail Road, Longmont, 80501; 303-651-8374. Offers appraisals the first Saturday of each October.

■ ARCHITECTURAL ARTIFACTS

Architectural Stuff, 3970 West Broadway, Englewood, 80110; 303-761-2999.

Castle Pines Antiques, 4700 Castleton Way, Castle Rock, 80104; 303-814-7880.

Raven Architectural Artifacts, 600 North Second Street, LaSalle, 80645; 970-284-0921.

Victorian Treasure, 3460 West Thirty-second Avenue, Denver, 80211; 303-480-0738; www.victoriantreasures.com.

■ CHINA AND GLASSWARE

Cobweb Shoppe, 28186 Main Street, Evergreen, 80439; 303-674-7833.

La Cache, 400 Downing Street, Denver, 80218; 303-871-9605.

COUNTRY ACCESSORIES, VICTORIANA, FOLK ART, AND PRIMITIVES

Different Drummer Antiques, 5465 Manhart Avenue, Sedalia, 80135; 303-688-0133.

Sharon's, 315 Mountain Avenue, Berthoud, 80513; 970-532-7071.

Painted Primrose, 149 B Second Avenue, Niwot, 80544; 303-652-0525.

Nan and David Pirnack, P.O. Box 489, Mead, 80541; 970-535-9343.

EUROPEAN AND WORLD

BlueCrate, 335 West Main Street, Trinidad, 81082; 719-846-4005; www.bluecrate.net. Asian rustic architectural artifacts and antiques, mostly Tibetan and East Asian.

Another Time, Another Place, 1181 South Street, Louisville, 80027; 720-890-7700; www.atapantiques.com. French.

The Apiary, 585 Milwaukee Street, Denver, 80206; 303-399-6017.

Black Tulip Antiques Ltd., 1370 South Broadway, Denver, 80210; 303-777-1370.

Ca Shi, 3458 Walnut Street, Denver, 80205; 303-297-2947. Asian.

DjUNA, 221 Detroit Street, Denver, 80206; 303-355-3500. Eclectic.

East–West Designs, 303 Josephine Street, Denver, 80206; 303-316-9520. Japanese.

Eron Johnson Antiques, Ltd., 451 Broadway, Denver, 80203; 303-777-8700; www.eronjohnsonantiques.com. World.

Indochine, 2525 Arapahoe Avenue, Boulder, 80302; 303-444-7734. Asian.

McKinley & Hill Antiques, 4340 Harlan Street, Wheat Ridge, 80033; 303-424-1102. English, American, and French.

Metropolitan Antiques Gallery, 1147 Broadway, Denver, 80203; 303-623-3333.

Paris Blue, 350 Kalamath Street, Denver, 80223; 720-932-6200.

Shaggy Ram, 0210 Edwards Village Boulevard, P.O. Box 2727, Edwards, 81632; 970-926-7377. French and English.

Sheilagh Malo Antiques, 1211 East Fourth Avenue, Denver, 80206; 303-777-3418.

Stuart–Buchanan Antiques Ltd., 1530 Fifteenth Street, Denver, 80202; 303-825-1222. Country European.

Suzan Dentry Antiques, 303-279-8776; www.suzandentryantiques.com. Wide selection of antiques and art.

Warner's Antiques, 1401 South Broadway, Denver, 80210; 303-722-9173; www.warnersantiques.com. Asian, European, and American.

■ EARLY AMERICAN

John Boulware Antiques, 1416 South Broadway, Denver, 80210; 303-733-7369.

Starr Antiques, 2940 East Sixth, Denver, 80206; 303-399-4537.

■ FINE ART

Antique Art, 285 South Milwaukee Street, Denver, 80209; 303-282-5950.

David Cook Fine American Art, 1637 Wazee Street, Denver, 80202; 303-623-8181; www.davidcookfineart.com.

Galerie Rouge, 2201 Larimer Street, Denver, 80205; 303-298-1848. Original vintage posters of the late nineteenth to mid-twentieth century.

Mary Williams Gallery, 2116 Pearl Street, Unit C, Boulder, 80302; 303-938-1588; www.thegreatartdoors.com.

Neal R. Smith Fine Art, P.O. Box 200008, Denver, 80220; 303-399-3119; www.finepaintings.com.

Saks Gallery, 3019 East Second Avenue, Denver, 80206; 303-333-4144.

Tam O'Neill Fine Art, 311 Detroit Street, Denver, 80206; 800-428-3826; www.tamoneillfinearts.com.

■ GARDEN

L&M Garden Center, 735 East Highway 56, Berthoud, 80513; 970-532-3232.

Birdsall & Co., 1540 South Broadway, Denver, 80210; 303-722-2535.

The West End Gardener, 777 Pearl Street, Boulder, 80302; 303-938-0607.

■ LIGHTING

Antique Lighting from Alden, 1454 South Broadway, Denver, 80210; 303-778-0634.

■ REPAIR AND RESTORATION

Denver Woodwrights, LLC, 3559 Brighton Boulevard, Denver, 80216; 303-777-2868.

Lockwood House, 198 Second Avenue, 1-C, Niwot, 80544; 303-652-2963.

Rejuvenation Fixtures, 2550 Northwest Nicolai Street, Portland, Oregon 97210; 888-401-1900; www.rejuvenation.com. Reproductions of period lighting and hardware.

RUGS

Castle Rugs, 565 Third Street Berthoud, 80513; 970-532-2187.

Shaver–Ramsey Oriental Rugs & Accents, 2414 East Third Avenue, Denver, 80206; 303-320-6363; www.shaver-ramsey.com.

Azari Rug Gallery, 1410 South Broadway, Denver, 80210; 303-744-2222; www.azari-rug.com.

Lewis Bobrick Antiques, 1213 East Fourth Avenue, Denver, 80218; 303-744-9203; www.lewisbobrickantiques.com.

RUSTIC AND MOUNTAIN

Little Bear Antiques & Uniques, 415 South Spring Street, Aspen, 81611; 970-925-3705.

Shepton's Antiques, 389 South Broadway, Denver, 80209; 303-777-5115. Rustic teak, pine, architectural.

Ski Country Antiques, 114 Homestead Road, Evergreen, 80439; 303-674-4666.

White Hart Gallery, 843 Lincoln Avenue, Steamboat Springs, 80487; 970-879-1015.

High Country Furniture & Gallery, Inc., 68 Ninth Street, Steamboat Springs, 80487; 970-879-2670.

Into The West, 807 Lincoln Avenue, Steamboat Springs, 80487; 970-879-8377.

SILVER (SEE SILVER CHAPTER)

Bedell & Co., 767 Pearl Street, Boulder, 80302; 303-939-9292, www.bedellandco.com.

McDowell's Antiques, 1400 South Broadway, Denver, 80210; 303-777-0601; www.mcdowellantiques.com.

WEBSITES

National Association of Collectors; www.collectors.org.

Antique and Collectibles Association; www.antiqueandcollectible.com.